7.

HOW TO FALL IN LOVE WITH TOFU

HOW TO FALL IN LOVE WITH TOFU

A (MOSTLY VEGETARIAN) COOKBOOK BY

Emma de Thouars

Smith
Street
Books

FOREWORD

A whole book about tofu – yes, really. When I tell people what I've been working on, I get a lot of surprised reactions. It seems especially difficult for everybody to imagine so many tofu recipes, an ingredient that plenty of people don't know what to do with. It was actually the other way around. There are forty recipes in this book, but it could easily have been a hundred. I had to cut quite a few. Tofu is crazily versatile and is eaten in many ways in many Asian countries: fried, steamed, raw, with sauces, in stews, hidden in pancakes or in dumplings. This is, therefore, not an all-encompassing bible – tofu is too diverse for that. In this book, I tell you how I prefer to prepare my tofu.

Good tofu has a soft and creamy texture. Its flavour is subtle, but certainly not boring; you should be able to taste the soybean, because that's what it's made of.

Tofu is the perfect canvas to soak up whatever flavours you throw into the pan. People often say that you have to know how to prepare it properly, but I snack on a lot of raw tofu while cooking, so I don't completely agree. In any case, I'll help you learn to prepare it; whether you eat raw tofu in the meantime is up to you.

Tofu is mainly seen as a meat substitute in the West, but people in Asia think of it differently. So do I. Sometimes tofu is eaten with meat,

so while most recipes in this book are vegetarian, some are not. In any case, I don't shy away from fish and oyster sauce, and sometimes a little minced (ground) pork or fish is added to a recipe. If so, I usually include an option to make the dish vegetarian. Sometimes not. You can use mushrooms or another alternative to make Tofu stuffed with minced pork (see page 79) or fish paste (see page 83), but you lose the heart of those dishes.

Tofu plays the leading role in all the recipes in this book, but of course you should also eat vegetables. I actually eat Broccoli with sesame oil (see page 155) alongside almost every dish, because it goes with everything. If you're a bit more adventurous than I am, I'll give you some other options at the end of this book for dressings and sauces that are delicious on different types of vegetables.

When you step into an Asian grocery store, the tofu offering is dizzying: firm, silken, soft, medium, egg and pudding. Each variety of tofu has its own method of preparation, but I'll help you there too: don't worry. Once you know what you're doing, I promise you'll love tofu as much as I do.

Lots of love and happy cooking,

Emma

DRIED BEAN CURD
(HARICOT CAILLE SECHE)

壹級三邊腐竹

INGREDIENTS: SOYA BEAN WATER
NET WT. 7oz (200 g.) (HARICOT ET EAU)

淨重七安士

Made in China   中國特產

PACKED BY: FOO YUEN LOONG FOODS FACTORY
LOT NO. 1726 IN D. D. 107 SHA PO,
YUEN LONG, N.T. HONG KONG.
FAX: 2482 1860   TEL: 2477 2018

中國東莞製造   富源隆食品廠運庄

Dynasty

嫩豆腐

TOFU SOFT

Net
Weight: 500gr

VERSE
TOFU

VOOR BAKKEN, STOMEN,
FRITUREN EN WOKKEN

250 gram

日本嫩清   Unicurd
豆腐   Silken tofu
Silky, Smooth & Springy

絹ごし

Net Weight: 300g

Unicurd

絹豆腐

Silken
tofu
Special

Smooth, Springy
& Delicate

TOFU 101

Before you get started, it's helpful if you know some ins and outs. Tofu seems simple, but it's quite a broad term. There are countless different types, so it's important that you know what you're buying and what you're doing with each kind.

All tofu is made from soy milk; the differences come from the way in which the tofu is made, what agent is added in its production and the amount of moisture the tofu contains. Firm tofu is made by adding magnesium chloride to the soy milk, which separates the curd from the whey (a bit like making cheese). You press the whey (the moisture) out of the tofu, and the more you squeeze out, the firmer the tofu becomes. Silk tofu is made with gypsum, which binds and stiffens the tofu, a bit like panna cotta.

I've included a recipe for homemade tofu on page 23. Don't be alarmed, it's much easier than you think and the results are mind-blowing. All recipes in this book have been further tested with store-bought tofu; personally, I don't make soy milk every day. There's absolutely no need to make your own tofu, except that it's one of the tastiest things you'll ever eat.

First things first, get started with the other recipes and, after a while, throw yourself into making your own tofu.

BUYING TOFU

Depending on where you live, the tofu available in the supermarket may not be the best: spongy, chewy and the reason many people think they don't like tofu. Here's what you should buy:

Firm tofu

The most famous type of tofu is firm tofu. This is also the kind you often find at the supermarket. If an Asian grocery store is accessible where you live, buy yours there; some sell fresh tofu, which you sometimes have to put in a bag yourself.

Firm tofu is often deep-fried or pan-fried until crispy before being incorporated into a sauce. Due to its sturdy structure, firm tofu does not fall apart easily. Deep-fried cubes of tofu with a pinch of salt on top are my favourite chef's treat. I sometimes crumble firm tofu to create a kind of mince (ground meat) texture; I'm not a fan of meat substitutes, but crumbled tofu is delicious with noodles or in dishes that you normally prepare with ground beef.

Soft tofu

Soft tofu is not sold at every shop, but it is perhaps my favourite because it has the perfect texture. Soft tofu falls between firm and silky tofu. It is firm enough to fry, but when you bite or cut it open, the structure is wonderfully jiggly and silky smooth. Just be careful: if you fry soft tofu and add it into a sauce, stir gently.

Silken tofu

Even softer is silken tofu. Silken tofu should not be deep-fried or subjected to any dry-heat cooking method because of its soft structure.

Silken tofu is delicious served cold with toppings (which also happens to be quick to make) or cut into cubes that you simmer in a sauce or stew so that the tofu absorbs all of the flavours. I always buy silken tofu from the Unicurd brand (look for the red packaging).

If you can't find Unicurd where you live, the Fortune brand also sells Japanese silken tofu (sometimes sold as a cylinder, sometimes as a square), which is even softer, if possible, and also suitable for any recipe that calls for silken tofu.

Tofu pudding

Douhua, tofa or tofu pudding is sold in large buckets in the refrigerated section of Asian grocery stores. It is often eaten as a dessert with syrup, or as a savoury snack with toppings.

Tofu pudding has almost the same texture as silken tofu, but is slightly softer. It's immensely satisfying to scoop a big spoon out of a freshly opened bucket, when the top is still beautifully smooth and shiny. Just be careful with transport; if you shake the bucket too much, you will come home with a mess.

Egg tofu

Egg tofu is made from soy milk with egg mixed in. Egg tofu originated in Japan, which is why it's sometimes called Japanese tofu. Stores may sell it as 'egg tofu', or as 'Japanese silken tofu'; the egg tofu that I always buy is called 'silken tofu special' (Unicurd).

Whatever it's called, you'll immediately recognise this variety because it's yellow. Egg tofu is almost always sold as a cylinder, which you cut into slices, deep-fry and then simmer in sauce. In terms of texture, it resembles soft tofu. Egg tofu is very smooth, but it's firmer than silken tofu so it can take a beating.

The flavour is different from soybean tofu: a bit eggier of course, but still very subtle. When it comes to taste, it's mainly about the sauce you serve it in.

Tofu skin

When you make soy milk, a skin forms on the milk – just like when you heat cow's milk. If you make tofu yourself, this skin is the tastiest snack ever, but it's also sold as dried sheets at Asian grocery stores. You can break the sheets up and stir them into soup – in broth, they become very soft and slippery. Or soak them in hot water for a few minutes, pat dry and fry until crispy for tofu crisps, like you do when making Nasi lemak (see page 120).

There are two types of tofu sheets available: one is slightly softer and the other firmer. You make the best crispies from the firm ones. You also have tofu knots, which are tofu sheets that are folded and tied. You can soak them in hot water, deep-fry them and dip them in a sauce of your choice (for example, the Korean fried tofu on page 134).

Other types of tofu

The varieties above cover the types of tofu I use in this book, but there are so many more. In Myanmar you have Shan tofu (named after the province of the same name), made from chickpea flour, and in Japan, there's goma tofu, made from sesame.

You can buy smoked tofu, which has a slightly meaty taste due to the smoky flavour – nice for stir-frying. At Asian grocery stores, you can also find jars of fermented tofu, which is sometimes used to stir-fry vegetables. I don't use these types in this book, but they are fun to try.

The world of tofu is endless!

Pressing
Many recipes tell you to press tofu first: cover it with paper towel, place something heavy on it and let it sit for a while. This way you squeeze out part of the moisture and the tofu becomes extra crispy when you fry it. I never actually do this. The reason I love tofu so much is because of its creaminess and soft consistency; you lose that when you squeeze the moisture out. For extra crispiness, you can always add a layer of cornflour (corn starch), or just fry for a long time at a high temperature, as I usually do.

Blanching
Tofu is often blanched briefly in boiling salted water before use. This removes the taste of the binding agent or coagulant, makes the tofu slightly firmer and gives it a light flavour. I never actually do this, because I find it a hassle. It does make tofu a bit tastier, so feel free to try.

Salting
Another way to flavour tofu before cooking is to salt it briefly. Cut the tofu into cubes or slices, arrange in a single layer and sprinkle with salt. Let sit while you prepare the rest of the ingredients (about 15 minutes). I'm usually too lazy for this, but Xinyu is specific about using this technique in her recipe for Sichuan barbecue tofu (see page 124).

Cutting
As with all ingredients, how you slice your tofu matters quite a bit. The bigger the blocks, the creamier the inside will be, while small cubes will turn out extra crunchy. In some recipes, I combine big and small blocks of tofu.

I give directions for cutting in every recipe, but if you go for it yourself, then you'll know what effect different cutting techniques will have on tofu.

Portions
The recipes in this book are sometimes for one, two to three, or four people. Not very consistent, but that's because I usually try to use up an entire block of tofu. Different types of tofu are sold in different sizes, and the amount of tofu you'll want to cook will also depend on whether you eat it by itself, with some vegetables and rice on the side, or as part of a larger meal. As you work through the recipes, you'll figure out how much to cook.

Measurements
I use measuring spoons for all the recipes in this book. These spoons are slightly larger than your standard spoons for eating. If you don't feel like buying some, at least keep the size difference in mind and use a dash or scoop extra.

1 tablespoon = 15 ml (½ fl oz)
1 teaspoon = 5 ml (¼ fl oz)

PANTRY

STAPLES

A well-stocked pantry is a must if you want to cook delicious Asian food at home. I always recommend building one little by little; no one needs to buy this whole list all at once. Start with a recipe and get what you need, see what else you can do with those ingredients, and then try another recipe. This way you expand slowly, and you don't end up with unnecessary ingredients that you only use once.

Rice

Almost all dishes in this book are best served with rice. Rice is the foundation for everything, so make sure you buy good-quality options and prepare your rice with love (see page 153). I always use pandan rice, which is often sold as jasmine rice. Always go to the market/grocer and look for a round, green Thai quality mark. Not every store sells the same brands, but if you see that logo, the rice will be good.

Pandan/jasmine rice is long grain, while in Japan and Korea, short-grain rice is popular. My favourite short-grain rice comes from Taiwan; if you find rice grown there, you should always buy it.

Can't make it to an Asian grocery store? Just make sure not to buy rice that comes in a cardboard package, because then your rice will also taste like cardboard. If possible, I would just buy very large bags of rice from Asian grocery stores: then you'll never run out.

Soy sauce

Besides rice (and tofu, of course), soy sauce is perhaps the most important ingredient in this book. A dash goes into almost every dish. In Chinese kitchens, you have a choice between light and dark soy sauce. I buy both from the Pearl River Bridge brand. Light soy sauce has a slightly saltier taste, while dark soy sauce is added mainly for colour. If you want to go all out, you can also buy Japanese, Korean or Thai soy sauce, but this is not really necessary.

Neutral oil

Most recipes call for neutral oil. By that, I mean oil that is neutral in taste with a high smoke point. Rice bran oil is my favourite, but sunflower, peanut, soybean and canola oils work just as well.

Salt

When I say salt, I mean fine salt. I also always have salt flakes at home to provide dishes with extra crunch. If a recipe needs flakes, I'll mention it specifically. If you prefer to use sea salt, that works as well.

MSG

A lot of people freak out when they see monosodium glutamate (MSG) in an ingredient list, thinking it's bad for you. That's not true. People think that it makes them bloated or gives them headaches. There is no evidence for this and these assumptions are based on (sorry) racist stereotypes. You don't hear anyone complaining while they stir stock cubes through their pasta sauce or eat a bite of Doritos.

The flavour enhancer MSG also occurs naturally in certain products, such as parmesan cheese. In Asian grocery stores, you can buy it as a white powder, and you only need to add a small pinch to a dish to give it a lot of flavour. MSG makes dishes extra savoury and addictive: it's basically instant umami. If you're sensitive to it, leave it out, but otherwise, get a bag to keep at home.

Chilli flakes

If there are dried chilli flakes in a recipe, I simply mean the same ones you use for spaghetti aglio e olio. You can make them yourself by roasting dried chillies in a dry frying pan and grinding them in a spice/coffee grinder or blender. These flakes are the tastiest, but store-bought is also good.

Gochugaru

These Korean chilli flakes are made from sun-dried chillies with the seeds removed. The taste is slightly milder and sweeter than the chilli flakes you may be used to – almost smoky too. So don't replace gochugaru with other chilli flakes: just get some, okay?

Crispy chilli oil

Chilli crisps are the crunchy bits of chilli flakes that are left over when you make chilli oil. Never throw them away! A spoonful of these on a bowl of rice with an egg, vegetables or noodles is delicious.

I have several types of crispy chilli oil at home. These are mostly homemade (see page 175), but some are store-bought, like Lao Gan Ma's. Flipping through this book, you might think that I get a lot of money from Lao Gan Ma, but that's not the case. The founder of this brand is one of the richest women in China: she doesn't need me at all. I give her every penny because Lao Gan Ma makes the very best ready-to-use chilli crisps. I always have their cripsy chilli oil and peanuts in chilli oil at home. The oil is nice to mix with sauces, the peanuts to scoop on dishes.

Sambal oelek

To make dishes spicier, you can add a spoonful of sambal oelek, even if a dish is not Indonesian. Sambal oelek consists of red chilli and salt, making it a great all-purpose source of spice. If I spoon sambal on or next to my food (as with the Nasi lemak on page 120) I buy sambal with extra ingredients added in. My favourite contains a lot of lime leaf. If you go to an Indonesian grocery store, they often sell homemade sambal.

Dried chillies

You can stew dried chillies in sauces or soups, but you can also stir-fry them in a dish. They give off a spicy aroma, which is less intense than a spoonful of chilli powder. There is quite a difference between varieties and sizes, but I think it's nonsense to buy a bunch of different chillies if you don't cook with them much. My favourite are Sichuan dried chillies; they are moderately spicy and go well with everything.

Sichuan chilli bean paste

A bit of Sichuan chilli bean paste can give your dish a lot of flavour. The beans are fermented together with chillies, which makes the beans very rich in taste, with a lot of depth.

Chilli bean paste is often sold as 'toban jiang' or 'douban jiang'. The best is made in the Sichuan town of Pixian, so look for this in the store. This paste contains fewer additives, but large pieces of beans, so you have to chop it up. Some brands are more user-friendly and sell it finely ground, so you can spoon it into the pan. All pastes are quite salty, so always taste before adding more salt to a dish.

Sichuan peppercorn oil

Sichuan peppercorn oil is made from Sichuan pepper and gives dishes just that little bit of depth and flavour without causing your mouth to tingle. You can buy the oil ready-made at Asian grocery stores, but I always make mine myself. On page 157, I explain how to do that.

Gochujang

The Korean chilli bean paste gochujang is a lot smoother, fresher and spicier than the Sichuan chilli bean paste mentioned above. It's delicious as a base for sauces and soups.

OTHER INGREDIENTS

Crispies
Almost every dish is improved by a handful of crispies. At the end of this book, I give you recipes for my favourites, but I also always have some ready-made crispies on hand – baked onions for example. I get a lot of crispies from the Indian grocery store, where they sell bhujia or sev, crispy noodles made from moth bean and/or chickpea flour. I usually get the plain versions, but they also sell spicy ones. There are also delicious ready-made crispies in the form of chickpeas or Bombay mix, in which everything (including crispy lentils) is mixed together.

Fermented black beans
By fermenting black soybeans with salt, you get a very salty, strong flavour that adds a lot of umami to your dishes. Fermented black beans are widely used in Chinese kitchens, but they come in handy everywhere. Always rinse the beans under the tap first so that they are a little less salty, unless I specifically advise you not to.

Ginger
The only fresh product in this list. I assume you know what it is and where you buy it, but I just want to tell you: you never have to peel it. I think it's pointless to peel ginger because you can't taste the difference.

Pickled mustard leaf
People often tell me that they can't find pickled mustard leaf. It's a product that comes in many forms, so I'll leave it up to you to pick one you'd like to buy.

Mustard leaf is pickled in salt, which gives it a very salty, slightly pickle-like taste. It is delicious in dishes cooked in woks, and also in sauces. I always buy mine chopped up, but you can also buy whole pieces in liquid that you cut up.

The taste is slightly different, but both work. Most Chinese grocery stores have a lot of different pickled vegetables, so if you can't find mustard leaf, just use another vegetable. It's about adding fermented goodness to your dish.

Katsuobushi
In Japanese cuisine, katsuobushi is widely used to add umami and depth to dishes. For example, you use the dried and shaved bonito flakes (bonito is a type of tuna) to make dashi (Japanese broth), but it is also delicious as a topping. A fun bonus: the flakes start to dance when you put them on something warm.

Kecap manis
This viscous Indonesian soy sauce comes in many shapes and sizes. My favourite is soy sauce medja, which falls between manis (sweet) and asin (salty) in taste. Look for a white, rectangular bottle with a green label and cap (Tjap Kaki Tiga).

Cornflour
Cornflour (corn starch) is often used to thicken sauces. Always mix cornflour with some water first to form a slurry. You then add that slurry to the already simmering sauce. This is so that you don't end up with lumps.

Noodles
I never really like standard wheat noodles, not even most of the ones from Asian grocery stores. I often choose dried udon noodles or noodles from the refrigerator (not the freezer!).

Oyster sauce / mushroom sauce
A favourite ingredient in Chinese kitchens, oyster sauce is thick and very concentrated in taste – you only need a little bit to give a dish a lot of flavour. If you are vegetarian, you can replace oyster sauce with mushroom sauce. I always buy the premium oyster sauce and mushroom vegetarian stir-fry sauce, both from Lee Kum Kee.

Sesame paste

To make dishes creamy and nutty, sometimes a little sesame paste is needed. At the Asian grocery store, you can buy Chinese sesame paste, which is slightly darker and thicker than Middle Eastern tahini. I think you can replace the two one-to-one (or even swap in peanut butter). Don't tell China.

Sesame oil

In terms of sesame oil, I don't necessarily have a favourite brand, but it's important that the oil doesn't contain a bunch of additives; always look at the ingredients list. Often, different types of oil are combined. All brands that say 100 per cent sesame on the bottle are good.

Tamarind

Tamarind is used a lot in Indonesian cooking. The pulp of the tamarind fruit has a sour taste, so if you don't have any at home, you can also add a squeeze of lemon juice.

You buy tamarind in blocks that you have to soak in hot water for a while. You can also buy tamarind paste in a jar, which you can simply spoon into your dish. I always tell you which one you need, but you can replace one with the other.

Tea

Nice to drink, but also to add flavour to dishes. If you can, use good-quality tea. I usually buy mine in Asia, but of course you can also go to a good tea shop. I always mention the specific tea I use, but you can switch things up with your favourites.

Black vinegar

Once you bring a bottle of this into your home, you can use it in everything. Black vinegar is also known as Chinkiang vinegar, named after the city where it comes from. The taste is malty and roasted, almost smoky but also slightly sweet. It's delicious as a dipping sauce for everything, or added into sauces. Look for a bottle with a yellow label – the cap is usually yellow but sometimes orange.

EQUIPMENT

Wok

You can't cook Asian food without a wok. And by a wok, I mean carbon steel or cast iron. Metal conducts heat much better, which is important when you're cooking with a wok.

In addition to stir-frying, I also use my wok for deep-frying. A good wok, provided you maintain it properly, becomes darker and more beautiful with age, the food you cook in it tastier.

For a new wok, first scrub the layer of factory oil with a scouring pad and dish liquid. Heat the wok over high heat and pour in a few tablespoons of neutral oil. Turn the wok in circles so that the oil covers the entire surface. Add roughly 5 cm (2 in) pieces of spring onion (scallion) and slices of ginger, and move them around the surface of the wok. Reduce the heat to medium and fry the spring onion and ginger for 15–20 minutes, continuing to move them around.

Remove the spring onion and ginger from the wok and rinse the wok with water – do not use detergent. Dry the wok by putting it over a low heat for 1–2 minutes, until all the water droplets have dried. After each use, rinse the wok with water, without detergent, and dry it immediately to prevent rusting. The more greasy food you prepare in the wok, the stronger the non-stick coating becomes. Acid or water affects this layer, but that's okay. If you notice that your food is sticking, repeat the process above.

Steamer or steamer basket

Steaming is one of the easiest ways to prepare food because you can just walk away while it's happening. My double-layer aluminium steamer is therefore one of my most prized possessions. You can easily fit two eggplants (aubergines) or a large bowl of steamed egg (see page 56) in it. You can also buy steamer baskets, but I find them a little less user-friendly.

Kitchen thermometer

A kitchen thermometer may cost a pretty penny but it is very useful, especially when deep-frying. Usually it doesn't matter much, but sometimes the temperature of the oil is very important.

There are other tricks to see how hot oil is (test with a piece of bread to see how quickly it browns, or stick a chopstick in the oil and see how rapidly it bubbles), but nothing gives you more certainty than a thermometer.

Skimmer

Also useful for deep-frying, especially for fishing deep-fried goodies out of the oil. Buy a fine-mesh one, otherwise peanut, soybean or garlic crispies will fall through.

Cooling rack

A wire rack is often the best way to drain greasy food. You can also always use paper towel, but the bottom of the food will get soggy again because it will start to steam due to heat. When you place ingredients on a wire rack, the air underneath helps to keep things crispy. You want that.

Microplane grater

All other graters are dwarfed by the Microplane. For such a small kitchen tool, it is relatively expensive, but it will last for years and is the best tool to perfectly grate garlic, ginger, lime zest or whatever. So just dig into your wallet.

Citrus press

With a citrus press you can easily extract twice as much juice from your lemon or lime. I have one of those yellow squeezers that you can easily use to squeeze half a lemon or lime. Indispensable.

Coffee grinder or mortar and pestle

For freshly ground Sichuan peppercorns, cumin seeds, tea powder or other things that you need to grind in small quantities, I prefer to use a coffee grinder. A mortar and pestle also works, but it will take a little more effort. Of course I have both, but in principle you only need one. A spice grinder works too.

Plastic squeeze bottle

Maybe not the biggest must, but I can't live without one. I usually have a plastic squeeze bottle (see the photo on page 15) next to my stove with neutral oil in it – generally rice bran oil. This allows me to measure and aim the oil precisely. You may not fully understand what I'm talking about yet, but once you use one, you'll thank me.

MAKE YOUR
OWN TOFU

HOMEMADE TOFU

MAKES: 300 G (10½ OZ)
PREP TIME: 30 MINUTES
WAITING TIME: 8–12 HOURS

200 g (7 oz) dried soybeans
2 teaspoons nigari (magnesium chloride)
50 ml (1¾ fl oz) hot water

EQUIPMENT
blender
muslin (cheesecloth)
kitchen thermometer (optional)
tofu mould or sieve
400 g (14 oz) tin of anything

I'll start this book with the most impressive recipe. Tofu is one of the most fun things to make yourself, especially because the end product is unparalleled. You can't get anything comparable in supermarkets – nothing comes close to the creamy, custard-like texture.

You may be a little nervous right now, but making tofu is actually quite easy; you don't even have to buy a tofu mould to get started. A sieve also works.

You can get soybeans at the supermarket, but I always use organic ones. Since they're the main ingredient in tofu, your beans should be good quality. In addition to soybeans, you also need nigari (you may have to buy this online). Nigari is magnesium chloride, which causes soy milk to curdle when you heat it and the curd to separate from the whey. You press the curd into a mould and squeeze out most of the moisture, until you're left with tofu that has just the right texture – a bit like how you make ricotta.

This is basically a recipe for 'firm' tofu, only a very soft version of it. I always make my tofu loose: so loose that you're almost afraid it will fall apart. You can make it firmer by adding more nigari or by leaving the tin on top of the tofu longer, to squeeze out more moisture. But I like soft the best.

You make silken tofu in a different way, with a different means to bind the soy milk. I've tried this before because I like to see how something is made, but for me, the difference from store-bought was barely detectable.

Homemade tofu tastes best when it is still slightly warm, and I wouldn't add it right away to other dishes. Instead, try it served with tasty toppings. My favourite combination is homemade tofu with Love elixir (see page 29), but the combinations I list on page 74 are all good too.

Covered in the refrigerator, the tofu will keep for a few days. Let it come to room temperature for an hour or so before serving.

Place the soybeans in a bowl, cover with cold water and soak for 8–10 hours. To check whether the beans are ready, you can break them in half with your fingers. The beans should be the same light colour all over, inside and out. When they're ready, drain the beans into a bowl, saving the water; you will use it to make soy milk.

Add the beans and 500 ml (2 cups) of the preserved water to a blender, and puree for 3–5 minutes, until the beans are finely blended and you have a substance that looks like a milkshake. Transfer this mixture to a large pan and add 800 ml (27 fl oz) of water. Add 150 ml (5½ fl oz) of water to the blender and leave it on for a while to incorporate any left-over bean mixture. Pour the contents of the blender into the pan.

Bring the pan's conents to a slow boil over medium–low heat until a foamy head forms. That foam head can grow quite high, so make sure the pan is big enough. Turn off the heat and, over a large bowl, drain the milk through

a muslin-lined sieve. Squeeze as much milk as you can through the muslin. (This will hurt your hands.) You can wait for it to cool down, but I'm impatient so I always put on rubber dish gloves. Pour 150 ml (5½ fl oz) of water into the cloth with the soy pulp and wring it out one last time.

Place the soy milk in a smaller saucepan, bring to the boil, then reduce the heat to low and simmer gently for 5 minutes. (The milk must boil first so that it can solidify after.) Turn off the heat and let the milk cool for 2–3 minutes. For those with a kitchen thermometer, the milk should ideally be 73°C (163°F). If a skin forms on the soy milk, eat it – it's the tastiest thing in the world.

Meanwhile, mix the nigari with 50 ml (1¾ fl oz) of hot water. Add the nigari mixture to the milk, stir gently, cover and let sit for 8 minutes, or until curds and whey are evident when passed through with a spoon.

Line a tofu mould or sieve with muslin. If using a mould, place it in a large roasting tin or sink.

If using a sieve, place it over a large bowl. Spoon the contents of the pan into the tofu mould or sieve. Most of the whey should now drain quickly through the muslin; you may have to wait a while until there is room in the mould or sieve again.

Fold the corners of the muslin to cover the top of the tofu. Put the lid on the tofu mould or place a container on the tofu in the sieve. Add a tin as a weight on the lid or in the container. Leave for 20 minutes.

Open the muslin and check if the tofu is firm enough. Otherwise, leave it for another 5 minutes. Carefully remove the tofu from the mould and transfer to a large bowl of cold water to firm up a little. It's okay if the tofu falls apart a bit. Soak it in the cold water for 30 minutes, then place on a plate and drain for another 15 minutes. Serve it at room temperature with a tasty topping: Love elixir on page 29, for example.

LOVE ELIXIR

Everyone should have a love potion in their repertoire – a sauce so delicious that anyone who tastes it will instantly love you. This is mine. The effect is greatest when you serve this perfectly salty and greasy, fresh and crunchy topping on Homemade tofu (see page 23).

SERVES: 3–4
PREP TIME: 30 MINUTES

2 tablespoons Peanut crispies
    (see page 172)
2 tablespoons chilli flakes
75 ml (2½ fl oz) neutral oil
15 g (½ oz) coriander (cilantro), leaves
    and stalks finely chopped
40 mint leaves, finely chopped
1 teaspoon light soy sauce
½ teaspoon sea salt flakes

EQUIPMENT
kitchen thermometer (optional)

Crush or chop the peanut crispies. I always do this by placing the side of a cleaver on top of the peanuts and giving it a whack. A mortar or chopping with a knife also works.

Place the chilli flakes in a heatproof bowl. Heat the oil in a saucepan over medium heat to 180°C (350°F); you can test if the oil is hot enough by tossing a piece of coriander into the pan. If the oil immediately starts to sizzle, you're good to go.

Pour the hot oil over the chilli flakes. When the oil and chilli bubble up, immediately add the coriander and mint, so that the oil cools down and the chilli flakes do not overcook and become bitter. Add the soy sauce, stir in the peanut crispies and season with the salt flakes. The sauce only gets better if you let it sit for a while, so no rush.

Spoon the sauce over homemade tofu, silken tofu or anything else you find in your fridge.

1

BREAKFAST & SANDWICHES

SCRAMBLED TOFU WITH CRISPY CHILLI

My standard weekend breakfast is bread with scrambled eggs, chilli crisp and something fresh: spring onion (scallion), coriander (cilantro), chives or a combination. Whatever I have at home at that moment. Now it sometimes happens that I don't have an egg at home, but I do have tofu. That actually works just as well.

People often put turmeric in scrambled tofu so that it turns yellow, just like eggs. I think that's nonsense. Tofu is very tasty on bread, even if it is white. Use soft tofu, which has the same texture as a perfectly soft scrambled egg. If you find chilli crisp a bit too intense for the morning, you can also eat this tofu on rice.

SERVES: 2
PREP TIME: 10 MINUTES

4 slices of sourdough bread
olive oil, for frying
1 tablespoon chilli crisp from Lao Gan Ma
200 g (7 oz) soft tofu, crumbled
½ teaspoon black vinegar
finely chopped chives, spring onion
    (scallion) and/or coriander (cilantro),
    leaves and stalks, to garnish

Cut the slices of bread as straight as possible so that they cook evenly. Heat a few tablespoons of olive oil in a frying pan and fry the bread in it for a few minutes over medium–low heat, until golden brown. If the bread is cooking unevenly, press down any parts that remain white with a spatula or kitchen tongs. Remove from the pan and place, cooked side up, on two plates.

Wipe the pan clean and heat the chilli crisp in it over medium–low heat, until you see it liquefy and start to bubble. Add the tofu, black vinegar and a pinch of salt, and let simmer over medium heat for a few minutes. Liquid should come out of the tofu: make sure this moisture evaporates. Cook until all the moisture has evaporated and the tofu is warmed through.

Spoon the finished tofu onto the slices of bread, finish with the chives, spring onion and/or coriander, and serve.

CONGEE WITH SPRING ONION-GINGER SAUCE AND PEANUT CRISPIES

Congee (Chinese rice porridge) is one of the best things to eat when it's grey outside, but with this fresh spring onion-ginger sauce, congee is also perfect for spring. Because congee is so deliciously soft, crispies are a must. I use Peanut crispies here (see page 172), but basically any type is fine. You can also use store-bought fried onions or bhujia (see pages 16 and 95).

If you can't find broken rice, you can also use regular jasmine rice. It has to cook a little longer, and the results are a little less creamy.

SERVES: 2
PREP TIME: 1 HOUR

6 cm (2½ in) piece of ginger
50 g (1¾ oz) broken jasmine rice
2 tablespoons Shaoxing rice wine
100 ml (3½ fl oz) homemade stock
    (optional; see pages 162–165)
1 spring onion (scallion), thinly sliced
    into rings
3 tablespoons neutral oil
1 tablespoon rice vinegar
200 g (7 oz) spinach
300 g (10½ oz) silken tofu, cut into
    small pieces
2 tablespoons Peanut crispies
    (see page 172)

EQUIPMENT
kitchen thermometer (optional)

Thickly slice half the ginger. In a saucepan, combine the sliced ginger with the rice, Shaoxing, stock (if using) and 650 ml (22 fl oz) of water (750 ml/3 cups, if not using stock). Bring to the boil, stir, reduce the heat to low and cover the pan. Simmer gently for about 45 minutes, until you have a soft, creamy rice porridge. Stir occasionally so that the congee does not stick to the pan. I like fairly loose and lumpy congee, but some people prefer it a bit thicker. See for yourself.

Meanwhile, thinly slice the second half of the ginger and place in a heatproof bowl with the spring onion. Heat the oil in a saucepan over medium heat to 180°C (350°F); you can test if the oil is hot enough by tossing a piece of spring onion into the pan. If the oil immediately starts to sizzle, it's ready. Pour the oil over the ginger and spring onion. Let cool slightly, then add the vinegar.

When the congee is ready, fish out the pieces of ginger. Add the spinach and stir until completely wilted, then stir in the tofu. Simmer gently for 1 minute to warm the tofu.

Divide the congee between two bowls, spoon over the spring onion-ginger sauce and finish with the peanut crispies.

SAMBAL TAHU GORENG SANDWICH

It is very important that you buy the perfect roll for this sandwich. It should be crunchy and nice and fluffy inside: a bit like the ones you get at a good bakery. So go to a good baker or, if your butcher has rolls, ask if you can buy individual ones. If you can't find any that work, this spicy, gooey tahu (Indonesian for tofu) is also delicious on rice.

SERVES: 4
PREP TIME: 45 MINUTES

½ long cucumber, thinly sliced
100 ml (3½ fl oz) white vinegar
1 tablespoon granulated sugar
1 teaspoon coriander seeds
1 red onion, thinly sliced into rings
150 ml (5 fl oz) boiling water
35 g (1¼ oz) tamarind pulp
1 shallot, roughly chopped
4 garlic cloves, thinly sliced
2 red chillies, thinly sliced into rings
neutral oil, for frying
400 g (14 oz) firm tofu, cut into small cubes
2 daun salam leaves (also known as
    Indonesian bay leaf, available at
    Asian grocery stores)
30 g (1 oz) palm sugar
1 tablespoon sambal oelek
2 tablespoons ketjap manis
4 long white rolls

EQUIPMENT
mortar and pestle or
food processor (optional)

If you feel like it, remove the seeds from the cucumber with a spoon. Mix the vinegar with the sugar and a pinch of salt, and stir until dissolved. Add the coriander seeds, onion and cucumber, and set aside while you prepare the rest of the ingredients. Stir occasionally to make sure everything is properly submerged. You can do this well in advance – the pickled onion and cucumber will taste even better.

Pour the boiling water over the tamarind in a heatproof bowl and let sit while you prepare the rest of the ingredients.

Grind the shallot, garlic and chilli together in a mortar, or blitz them in a food processor; if you don't have either, you can simply chop the ingredients as finely as possible.

Heat a thick layer of neutral oil in a wok or frying pan over high heat and fry the tofu for 8 minutes, until golden and crispy. Remove from the pan and set aside.

Drain the oil from the wok or pan, leaving 2 tablespoons, and reduce the heat slightly. Fry the shallot, garlic and chilli mix for about 2 minutes. Mash the tamarind with a spoon in the water, then add to the pan with the daun salam, palm sugar, sambal oelek, ketjap manis and crispy tofu. Turn the heat back up to high and cook until the sauce is reduced and thick, about 3 minutes.

Cut the rolls in half, top with the onion, cucumber and tofu, and serve.

TOFU SANDO

A Japanese egg sando with egg salad and Kewpie mayonnaise is not difficult to make, but it's even easier if you make it with tofu. That way, you don't even have to boil and peel eggs; it's just a matter of mashing tofu and mayo together. Don't have Kewpie mayonnaise at home? Then add some extra rice vinegar.

SERVES: 2
PREP TIME: 10 MINUTES

250 g (9 oz) soft or firm tofu

10 g (¼ oz) chives, finely chopped

½ teaspoon Japanese mustard powder (available at Asian grocery stores)

3 tablespoons Kewpie mayonnaise

1 teaspoon rice vinegar

white pepper

4 slices of white bread, crusts removed

Place the tofu in a bowl and mash it with a fork. The tofu doesn't have to be finely mashed — just broken up into pieces.

Mix the chives, mustard powder, mayonnaise and rice vinegar through the tofu. Taste and season with salt and white pepper.

Fill the bread with the tofu to make two sandwiches, cut in half and serve.

BUTTER TOFU SLOPPY JOES

As a kid, one of my favourite movies was *It Takes Two*, featuring the Olsen Twins experiencing all sorts of drama at summer camp. The absolute highlight of the film is the scene where all the kids get sloppy Joes for dinner: a soft bun with saucy minced (ground) beef that drips down everyone's hands. So very sloppy. That sandwich seemed so magical and wonderfully American, but of course my parents would never make it for me. So I'll do it myself. My sloppy Joe is completely bastardised with tofu minced (ground) 'meat' and butter chicken flavours, but it's just as gooey as the ones from the movie, and that's what really matters.

SERVES: 4
PREP TIME: 15 MINUTES

60 g (2 oz) butter + extra for spreading
2 garlic cloves, finely chopped
3 cm (1¼ in) piece of ginger, finely chopped
¼ teaspoon chilli powder
½ teaspoon ground cumin
½ teaspoon garam masala
2 tablespoons tomato paste
    (concentrated puree)
250 g (9 oz) firm tofu, roughly broken up
125 ml (½ cup) double (heavy) cream
4 white or brioche buns
1 bunch of coriander (cilantro), stems and
    leaves finely chopped

Heat the butter in a frying pan over medium–low heat and fry the garlic and ginger for about 1 minute, until fragrant. Add the chilli powder, cumin and garam masala and fry for 30–60 seconds, until fragrant. Add the tomato paste and fry for 1 minute.

Add the tofu, cream and 120 ml (4 fl oz) of water. Bring to the boil, reduce the heat and let simmer gently for 5–10 minutes, until the flavours have infused the tofu and most of the moisture has evaporated. Don't let the tofu dry out; the butter tofu should be juicy without running off the bun.

Meanwhile, cut the buns in half and spread with butter. Toast them in a frying pan for a few minutes until golden brown and crispy (brioche cooks a little faster because it contains a lot of sugar).

Spoon the butter tofu onto the buns, sprinkle with plenty of coriander and serve.

TOFU & EGG

TAHU TELOR WITH EGGPLANT

Tahu telor is a Javanese omelette filled with tofu and, most importantly, an insanely delicious sauce that you will want to eat on everything. The main ingredient for that sauce is petis udang, a syrupy prawn (shrimp) paste. This absolutely cannot be replaced by belacan, because belacan does not have the flavour that makes this recipe's sauce so tasty. In addition to tofu, I also stir in steamed eggplant (aubergine) so there are some extra vegetables, though I often eat broccoli with tahu telor. I also usually eat it with rice, though it's delicious on a sandwich the day after.

SERVES: 2–3
PREP TIME: 40 MINUTES

Omelette

150–200 g (5½–7 oz) Chinese
    eggplant (aubergine)
3 eggs
150 g (5½ oz) firm tofu, cut into 5 mm
    (¼ in) cubes
5 sprigs of coriander (cilantro), finely
    chopped + extra for garnish
neutral oil, for frying
¼ long cucumber, finely sliced

Sauce

100 g (3½ oz) peanuts
1 garlic clove, roughly chopped
1 red chilli, roughly chopped
1 tablespoon petis udang
2 tablespoons ketjap medja or manis
1 tablespoon palm sugar syrup
1 teaspoon tamarind paste

EQUIPMENT
steamer or basket
food processor

Preheat the oven to 170°C (340°F). Roast the peanuts in the oven for 15–20 minutes, tossing occasionally, until they are browned all the way through; you can test if they are ready by cutting one open. The outside of the peanuts should be be dark but not burnt.

Meanwhile, bring water to the boil in a steamer or large saucepan with a steamer basket. Cut the eggplant into pieces that are small enough to fit inside your steamer or basket, and steam them for 10–15 minutes, until tender. (Chinese eggplants cook a little quicker.) After steaming, cut the eggplant into small cubes and drain in a colander while you prepare the rest of the ingredients

To make the sauce, grind the garlic, chilli and peanuts in a small food processor. The mixture doesn't have to be completely fine: it can still contain chunky pieces of peanut. Transfer to a saucepan and add the petis udang, ketjap, palm sugar syrup, tamarind and 100 ml (3½ fl oz) of water. Bring to the boil, then reduce the heat to medium and simmer for 3–5 minutes, until the sauce has reduced slightly and is nice and thick. Turn off the heat and set aside.

For the omelette, beat the eggs in a large bowl and season with salt. Stir in the tofu, eggplant and coriander. Heat a few tablespoons of oil in a frying pan over medium heat. Add the egg mixture, cover the pan and reduce the heat to low. Cook the omelette for about 10 minutes, until the top is cooked through.

You can flip the omelette to colour the other side; let it slide onto a large plate or the lid of the pan. Place the pan upside down on the omelette (make sure there is not much oil left in the pan) and flip it.

When the omelette is done, place it on a large plate and spoon over the sauce. Cover the centre with the cucumber and coriander to serve.

TOFU OMELETTE WITH TOMATO CHILLI SAUCE

This egg dish is wonderfully spicy and comforting at the same time. First, you first make a chilli sauce with charred tomatoes and chillies: a bit like a Mexican salsa, but with fermented black beans added in. By pouring that sauce into the egg when it is still partially liquid, you get an almost stew-like, saucy egg. With tofu, of course. If you don't have gas, you can also chargrill the tomato and chillies in a very hot, dry pan – preferably cast iron, if you have it. Let the pan get really, really hot.

SERVES: 2–3
PREP TIME: 25 MINUTES

Sauce

1 tomato

2 red chillies

1 small garlic clove, finely chopped

1 cm (½ in) piece of ginger, finely chopped

2 tablespoons crispy chilli oil (see page 175) or use Lao Gan Ma

1 tablespoon fermented black beans, chopped

Egg

4 eggs

neutral oil, for frying

300 g (10½ oz) silken tofu, cut into 3 cm (1¼ in) cubes

1 spring onion (scallion), finely chopped into rings

lots of cilantro (coriander), leaves and stalks finely chopped

EQUIPMENT

blender or immersion blender

For the sauce, roast the tomato and chillies directly on the flame of your gas stove, if you have one. Turn regularly, until their outsides are blackened. If you don't have a gas stove, you can do this in a very hot, dry frying pan.

Place the tomato and chillies (without stems) in a small blender or in the bowl of an immersion blender. Add the garlic, ginger and chilli oil and mash, then stir in the fermented black beans. Taste and season with salt, if necessary. (If you use my homemade chilli oil, you don't need to add any.)

Beat the eggs and season with a pinch of salt. Heat a layer of oil in a frying pan over medium heat. Pour the egg into the pan and wait until the bottom has set but the top is still runny. Distribute the tofu evenly over the pan, making sure that all the pieces are hugged by egg. Add the sauce with a small splash of water and simmer gently for 5 minutes, until the egg has set on top.

Once the egg is ready, garnish with the spring onion and cilantro, and serve in the pan.

EGG TOFU WITH MINCED PORK

This is the only egg tofu dish in this book, and I absolutely love it. The texture is very soft and custard-like, which makes sense considering it contains egg. Egg tofu is perfect for deep-frying and then simmering briefly in a sauce, so it's also delicious in the recipe for Spicy tofu with egg on page 61.

I don't eat much meat, but when I do, it's usually along these lines. A little bit of pork is more than enough here; it provides just enough fat and flavour. If you don't eat meat, you can replace the pork with mushrooms.

SERVES: 2
PREP TIME: 15 MINUTES

neutral oil, for frying

300 g (10½ oz) egg tofu, cut into 2 cm (¾ in) slices

50 g (1¾ oz) fatty minced (ground) pork (see tip)

1 garlic clove, finely chopped

1 cm (½ in) piece of ginger, finely chopped

2 tablespoons crispy chilli oil (see page 175) or use Lao Gan Ma

1 teaspoon cornflour (corn starch)

1 spring onion (scallion), finely sliced into rings

EQUIPMENT
kitchen thermometer (optional)

Heat a generous layer of oil in a wok or frying pan over high heat. The oil should be really hot, for a nice crispy layer around the tofu; if you have a thermometer, aim for 190–200°C (375–400°F); a cube of bread dropped in the oil will brown in 5–10 seconds.

Fry the egg tofu for 4–5 minutes, until golden brown, then drain on a wire rack or paper towel. If the pan is too small, fry the tofu in batches.

Drain the oil from the wok or frying pan, leaving 1–2 tablespoons. Add the minced pork and fry over medium heat for 4–5 minutes, until browned and starting to get crispy. Add the garlic and ginger and fry for 1–2 minutes, until fragrant. Add the crispy chilli oil and stir.

Meanwhile, mix the cornflour with 100 ml (3½ fl oz) of water. Add the mixture to the pan and let it simmer gently until the sauce thickens slightly, about 1 minute. Return the tofu to the pan and simmer for a further 1 minute, until the flavours have infused.

Serve with the spring onion on top.

MAKE VEGETARIAN: replace the minced pork with 200 g (7 oz) of shiitake mushrooms, chopped into 2–5 mm (⅛–¼ in) pieces. Shiitake mushrooms need more oil and a little more time than pork (8–10 minutes).

MINCED PORK TIP: depending on where you live, not every butcher has minced pork, but you can call in advance. You want nice and greasy minced meat, with those white bits in it. If the butcher doesn't have any, you can buy sausages and take out the meat; keep in mind that sausage has already been seasoned with salt and pepper.

STEAMED EGG WITH TOFU

I will forever have a soft spot for steamed egg. The texture is the perfect combination of soft, jiggly and light, but also just a little greasy. Every time I eat it with rice, I feel happy all over again. Better yet, it takes almost no effort because you just put the eggs in a steamer or basket and then you can lie on the couch.

At Fook Sing in Amsterdam, I ate steamed egg with silken tofu for the first time. The version I ate there – made with only egg whites and prawn (shrimp) on top – was totally insane. My recipe has more Japanese flavours, like dashi and nori. It's reminiscent of one of my other favourite quick meals: rice with a fried egg and roasted nori. The egg yolk with rice and nori is really magic, and this dish has a bit of that to it as well.

SERVES: 2–3
PREP TIME: 35 MINUTES

3 eggs
200 ml (7 fl oz) dashi (see page 165 or use
    store-bought instant dashi powder)
300 g (10½ oz) silken tofu, cubed
2 nori sheets (see tip)
1 tablespoon Japanese or light soy sauce
1 spring onion (scallion), thinly sliced
    into rings

EQUIPMENT
steamer or basket
plastic wrap
kitchen tongs

Bring water to the boil in a steamer or a saucepan with a steamer basket.

Place the eggs, dashi and a pinch of salt (if needed) in a bowl; if you use dashi powder, you can leave the salt out. Beat the eggs, then pass the mixture through a sieve to make it extra soft.

Carefully fold the tofu into the egg. Pour the mixture into a bowl, cover with plastic wrap and steam until the top is set but the egg is still jiggly. It takes me 25 minutes, but this depends on the shape of your bowl.

Meanwhile, grab a nori sheet with kitchen tongs and hold it just above the flame of your stove. You will see the nori getting a little crispy. Once the sheet is crispy all over, it's ready. If it catches fire now and then, don't panic – just blow out the fire and carry on.

Remove the egg from the steamer or basket and top with the soy sauce and spring onion. Serve the nori on the side so that it remains crispy until the last moment.

NORI TIP: if you don't have a gas stove, you can roast nori in a dry frying pan. Most Asian grocery stores also sell roasted nori as a snack. I like the texture of freshly roasted nori better, but the ready-to-eat versions are seasoned. There is something to be said for that.

MAKE VEGETARIAN: dashi contains katsuobushi, which is fish. To make this dish vegetarian, use Vegan dashi (see page 165).

SPICY TOFU WITH EGG

Sometimes, when I'm really lost for inspiration, I type in Chinese characters for ingredients on YouTube and see what comes up. The advantage is that I discover much tastier and more authentic recipes. The disadvantage is that I often do not understand what exactly goes into them. The first video I watched when I searched for 豆腐 (tofu) was something a bit like this dish. No idea if it tastes like the recipe in the Chinese video, but it sure is tasty.

SERVES: 3
PREP TIME: 30 MINUTES

500 g (1 lb 2 oz) soft tofu
2 eggs
neutral oil, for frying
3 garlic cloves, finely chopped
3 cm (1¼ in) piece of ginger, finely chopped
2 spring onions (scallions), finely sliced
    into rings
1 tablespoon sambal oelek
2 tablespoons light soy sauce
1 tablespoon black vinegar
1 teaspoon granulated sugar
2 tablespoons oyster sauce or
    mushroom sauce
1 teaspoon cornflour (corn starch)

Cut the tofu in half lengthways and then into slices about 1 cm (½ in) thick. Beat the eggs in a shallow bowl and carefully fold in the tofu so that it is coated on all sides – really carefully, though, otherwise the tofu will break.

Heat a generous layer of oil in a wok or frying pan over medium heat and fry the tofu for about 4 minutes, until golden brown. Do this in batches, if necessary. Drain the tofu on paper towel and wipe the pan clean.

Heat a few tablespoons of oil in the pan over medium–low heat and fry the garlic, ginger and white part of the spring onion for 1–2 minutes, until fragrant. Add the sambal oelek and fry for 1 minute. Add the soy sauce, black vinegar, sugar and oyster sauce or mushroom sauce and stir.

Meanwhile, mix the cornflour with 100 ml (3½ fl oz) of water. Add to the pan, then return the tofu to the pan and toss gently so you don't break it. Let the sauce simmer for 3–5 minutes until it has mostly reduced and the sauce has soaked into the tofu. Taste and season with salt.

Serve with the green part of the spring onion on top.

2

SNACKS

TOFU DUMPLINGS WITH SPRING ONION-GINGER CHILLI OIL

I don't make them very often anymore because I'm lazy, but dumplings remain the ultimate Asian snack. Feel free to make your own wrappers – because of the aforementioned laziness, I go for ready-made ones. I like wonton wrappers because they're so slippery, but you can also use other wrappers or make gyoza with the filling. As long as you serve the dumplings with this fabulous chilli oil, little can go wrong. The sauce is about double what you need, but it's also delicious on rice with a fried egg or noodles, or on cold silken tofu or tofu pudding with some crispies. The filling is also delicious on rice. Serve it cold, or fry it up in the pan with sesame seeds.

MAKES: 40 DUMPLINGS
PREP TIME: 45 MINUTES

Chilli oil

3 spring onions (scallions), thinly sliced
    into rings
1 garlic clove, grated
3 cm (1¼ in) piece of ginger, grated
1 teaspoon granulated sugar
½ teaspoon salt
25 g (1 oz) gochugaru
200 ml (7 fl oz) neutral oil
2 tablespoons black vinegar
1 tablespoon light soy sauce

Dumplings

400 g (14 oz) Napa cabbage, sliced into
    wafer-thin strips
1 teaspoon salt
250 g (9 oz) firm tofu, finely crumbled
1 tablespoon light soy sauce
1 tablespoon Shaoxing rice wine
1 teaspoon sesame oil
white pepper
40 wonton wrappers (thawed)

EQUIPMENT
kitchen thermometer (optional)
plastic wrap

Place the spring onion, garlic and ginger in a heatproof bowl. Add the sugar, salt and gochugaru.

Heat the oil in a saucepan over medium heat to 180°C (350°F). Test if the oil is hot enough by tossing a piece of spring onion in. If the oil immediately starts to sizzle, it's ready. Pour the oil evenly over the ingredients in the bowl and stir. Let cool to room temperature, then add the black vinegar and soy sauce.

Place the cabbage in a large bowl and add the salt. Massage the salt into the cabbage for a few minutes, until the cabbage shrinks. Squeeze out the moisture. Transfer to a sieve, squeeze the cabbage again and let it drain. Place it back in the bowl and add the tofu, soy sauce, Shaoxing, sesame oil and a pinch of white pepper. Mix well.

Prepare a small bowl of water. Place a wonton wrapper on your hand and fill it with about 1 teaspoon of filling. Wet the edges of the sheet with your finger, fold the corners together and pinch to close. Place on a plastic wrap–covered cutting board, and repeat with the rest of the filling.

See next page

Bring a large pot of generously salted water to the boil. Boil the dumplings for about 3 minutes, until heated through. Cook them in batches, if necessary; the dumplings are quite fragile, so you don't want them too close together. Don't overcook, or they will fall apart.

While the dumplings are cooking, put a scoop of the oil on a deep plate and spread it around a little. Remove the dumplings from the water and transfer to the plate; make sure only a little cooking water comes along with them.

Spoon some extra oil over the dumplings and serve.

FREEZING TIP: homemade dumplings in the freezer are a huge luxury. Place them on a cutting board covered with plastic wrap, making sure they are not touching each other, and freeze. When the dumplings are completely frozen, you can put them in a ziplock bag.

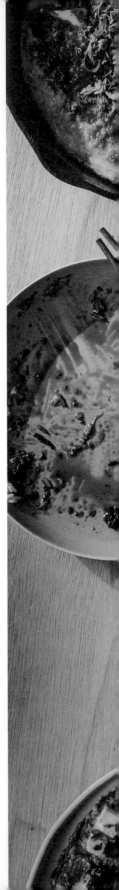

SNACKS

KOREAN TOFU PANCAKES
WITH PRAWNS

These Korean tofu pancakes (dubu jeon) are a deliciously greasy snack. I first ate them at a Korean tofu restaurant that specialises in Jiigae (see page 96), where you could order these treats as an appetiser. This recipe has a fairly chunky and messy batter, but that's what makes it so good. Because you have chunks of prawn (shrimp) and tofu, you get a lot of different textures and extra crunchy bits. So don't be disappointed if your pancakes aren't the prettiest, they're probably the tastiest. You can crumble them a bit and eat them on rice with some vegetables, and they're delicious cold the next day.

MAKES: 6–8 PANCAKES
PREP TIME: 20 MINUTES

MAKE VEGETARIAN: easy. Leave the prawn (shrimp) out.

100 g (3½ oz) prawns, peeled and deveined, chopped into small pieces
250 g (9 oz) firm tofu, crumbled into small pieces
2 spring onions (scallions), thinly sliced into rings
1 tablespoon gochugaru
2 eggs
2 tablespoons all-purpose flour
½ teaspoon salt
white pepper
neutral oil, for frying

Sauce
50 ml (1¾ fl oz) light soy sauce
50 ml (1¾ fl oz) rice vinegar
1 tablespoon toasted sesame seeds

EQUIPMENT
kitchen thermometer (optional)

In a large bowl, mix the prawns with the tofu, spring onion, gochugaru, eggs, flour, salt and a pinch of white pepper.

Heat a generous layer of oil in a frying pan over high heat to 180°C (350°F). You can test if the oil is hot enough by tossing a piece of spring onion into the pan. If the oil immediately starts to sizzle, you're good to go.

Spoon three chunks of batter into the pan and use two spoons or spatulas to form small discs. Fry the pancakes for 2–3 minutes per side, until the outside is golden brown – be careful when flipping. Let the pancakes drain on a wire rack or paper towel, and repeat with the rest of the batter.

Meanwhile, make the dipping sauce by mixing the soy sauce, rice vinegar and sesame seeds in a bowl.

Serve the pancakes with the dipping sauce.

AGEDASHI TOFU

Agedashi tofu is fried tofu served in a dashi-based broth. The nice thing about this is that part of the crispy layer of the tofu gets a little soggy, and part stays crunchy. Normally this dish is served with katsuobushi, but recently I had a version at a ramen restaurant in which the shaved bonito flakes were deep-fried with the tofu. This changes the taste completely and you get delicious, crispy layers. In addition, it looks very chic and takes no effort at all. I love that.

SERVES: 3–4
PREP TIME: 30 MINUTES

125 ml (½ cup) dashi (see page 165 or use
    store-bought instant dashi powder)
2 tablespoons Japanese or light soy sauce
2 tablespoons mirin
½ tablespoon granulated sugar
30 g (1 oz) fresh ginger
50 g (1¾ oz) daikon radish
2 spring onions (scallions), finely chopped
500 g (1 lb 2 oz) soft tofu, cut into 3 cm
    (1¼ in) cubes
50 g (1¾ oz) cornflour (corn starch)
10 g (¼ oz) katsuobushi
neutral oil, for frying

Stir the dashi, soy sauce, mirin and sugar in a saucepan over low heat until the sugar dissolves. Set aside.

Against my advice in the book's introduction, peel the ginger. Normally this isn't necessary, but because this recipe uses ginger that's very finely grated and eaten raw, you don't want any peel. Grate the ginger with the finest grater you have, and repeat with the radish. Rinse the spring onion under the cold tap; this makes it crisper.

Put the cornflour and katsuobushi in two different bowls, and season the cornflour with a pinch of salt. Dip the tofu in the cornflour first, then the katsuobushi. Wait a few moments for the cornflour to soak in a bit and repeat this process one more time: this way, you get an extra crispy and flaky layer. Heat a generous layer of neutral oil in a wok or frying pan over medium heat and fry the tofu for 6 minutes, until the katsuobushi is wonderfully crispy. Drain on a wire rack.

Divide the tofu between serving bowls and pour over the sauce. Place the ginger, radish and spring onion on top and serve. Eat quickly, otherwise the tofu will become soggy (though a little sogginess is tasty).

MAKE VEGAN: omit the katsuobushi and make a vegan dashi with kombu and shallots, like one on page 165, or with kombu and dried mushrooms, if you prefer.

SAUCE TIP: you can also buy ready-made tsuyu sauce at Asian grocery stores. You can heat it up and pour it over the tofu, which saves you from making a sauce.

EGGPLANT TIP: usually, while I'm at it, I double the sauce. Make slits in an eggplant (aubergine) and fry until done. Pour the sauce on top while the eggplant is still hot and refrigerate for a few hours for the perfect dish to serve with this tofu.

SILKEN TOFU WITH YUZU AND KATSUOBUSHI

Hiyayakko is cold silken tofu with Japanese-style toppings. It's the ideal snack on hot days because it's wonderfully refreshing and doesn't require heat to prepare. In terms of toppings, you can go in all directions: think spring onion (scallion), ginger, shiso leaves, radish or sesame seeds. Hiyayakko is almost always prepared with soy sauce, to which I add a little yuzu juice, but that's not necessary. You can also use ponzu. If you have expensive soy sauce, now is the time to get it out. In most dishes, I think it's a waste to use nice soy sauce, but because this one is so basic, you can really taste the soy sauce's quality. Other tasty toppings include millennial egg, spring onion and soy sauce, and peanuts in crispy chilli with spring onion or coriander (cilantro). Or spoon over the coriander sauce from page 90, the spring onion-ginger chilli oil from page 67 or the spicy sauce from page 95.

SERVES: 2–3
PREP TIME: 5 MINUTES

300 g (10½ oz) silken tofu
1 spring onion (scallion), thinly sliced
    into rings
½ teaspoon grated ginger
2 tablespoons Japanese or light soy sauce
1 tablespoon yuzu juice (available at Asian
    grocery stores)
handful of katsuobushi

Remove the tofu from the packaging and place it on a plate so that it can drain. Meanwhile, mix the spring onion with the ginger in a bowl. In another, mix the soy sauce with the yuzu juice.

Pour the water that has drained from the tofu off the plate (hold the tofu with your hand so that it does not fall into the sink). Place the spring onion and ginger on the tofu, and carefully pour over the sauce. Finish with a handful of katsuobushi and serve.

STUFFED
TOFU

TOFU STUFFED WITH MINCED PORK

Many people see tofu as a meat substitute, but tofu is often eaten with meat. This stuffed tofu comes from Chinese Hakka kitchens and is wonderfully saucy and comforting. Sometimes the tofu is deep-fried, but you can make it with a little less oil. You first fry the tofu till it's crispy and then add sauce so that it becomes soft again. That sounds unnatural, but crispy gone soggy is one of the tastiest textures – just try it. Dried mushrooms are often added, but I always forget to soak them in time and this dish is tasty enough without them.

I crumble the tofu you cut out and mix it with the minced (ground) beef. That's not how this dish is supposed to be made, but otherwise I think it's a waste of tofu. You can also use the ugly tofu pieces for Scrambled tofu with crispy chilli (see page 35).

SERVES: 2
PREP TIME: 20 MINUTES

neutral oil, for frying

Tofu
250 g (9 oz) firm tofu
2 spring onions (scallions), 1 finely
    chopped, 1 finely sliced into rings
100 g (3½ oz) minced (ground) pork
1 teaspoon cornflour (corn starch)
1 teaspoon grated ginger
1 tablespoon light soy sauce
¼ teaspoon sesame oil

Sauce
1 teaspoon cornflour (corn starch)
1 tablespoon light soy sauce
1 tablespoon oyster sauce
½ teaspoon granulated sugar
pinch of salt

Cut the tofu into 2 cm (¾ in) slices and cut those in half, into squares. Cut a square out of the tofu pieces with a small knife, taking care not to cut all the way through the tofu. Crumble the tofu you remove in a bowl.

Mix the chopped spring onion, minced pork, cornflour, ginger, soy sauce, sesame oil and a pinch of salt in the same bowl. Mix well for a few minutes; you want the fat in the mince to 'break' and the mince to almost become a paste, with some threads of fat running through it. You'll see what I mean if you stir long enough.

Fill the tofu with the minced meat mixture: the meat should rise slightly above the tofu in a small ball.

Mix all the ingredients for the sauce with 100 ml (3½ fl oz) of water and set aside. Heat a layer of oil in a wok or frying pan over medium heat and fry the tofu, mince side down, for 4 minutes. Turn the tofu over and fry for a further 4 minutes, until crispy. Stir the sauce well so that the cornflour is evenly mixed, then add to the pan and cover. Steam for about 5 minutes, or until the mince is cooked through. Remove the lid from the pan and let the sauce simmer for 1 minute, until it has reduced a bit.

Place the tofu on a plate or platter and spoon the sauce over it. Sprinkle over the spring onion rings and serve.

INARI SUSHI

I spent my whole life thinking that those sweet sushi rice wrappers were made of egg. Well think again: inari is made from tofu. Fortunately, you don't have to prepare the wrappers yourself; they're available ready-made at Asian grocery stores, sweet sauce and all. You only have to fill them with sushi rice. My filling came from things I had at home, but you can also mix other stuff into the rice, such as tuna, chives, sesame seeds, furikake – whatever you want. Fish roe on top make the inari nice and decadent (I use herring, salmon or trout roe), but this is totally optional. You'll make a little more rice than you need; I snack on a lot of the fillings while making these, and I have anticipated that you will too.

MAKES: 12 PIECES
PREP TIME: 45 MINUTES

200 g (7 oz) steamed short-grain rice
    (see page 153)
neutral oil, for frying
75 g (2¾ oz) shiitake mushrooms (or other
    mushrooms), chopped into small cubes
2 eggs
1 tablespoon mirin
1 tablespoon sake
1 teaspoon granulated sugar
4 shiso leaves, finely chopped, or 1 cup
    shiso cress (see tip)
45 ml (1½ fl oz) sushi vinegar (see tip)
12 inari bags (available at Asian
    grocery stores)
fish roe (rather expensive, so
    totally optional)
sushi ginger, to serve
wasabi, to serve

Heat a few tablespoons of oil in a wok or frying pan and fry the mushrooms with a pinch of salt for 5 minutes, until soft and cooked through; they don't need to darken much.

Meanwhile, in a bowl, beat the eggs with the mirin, sake, sugar and a pinch of salt. Remove the mushrooms from the pan with a slotted spoon, set aside, and fry the egg. It's best if the pan is large enough for the egg to cook in one thin layer, but if not, that's okay. Fry the egg until the top is set and remove it from the pan. Roll the egg up, slice it into thin strips, and slice those into pieces.

Mix the shiso leaves or cress, sushi vinegar, egg and mushrooms through the rice. Taste and add more vinegar, if needed.

Put the inari bags in a pan with the liquid that comes in the package, and warm them up a bit over low heat; this makes them easier to open. Carefully open one, making sure that it does not tear. Carefully fill with the rice. If you serve the inari with the closed side up, make sure that they're nicely stuffed and the rice is pressed down. This looks nicer. Fold the bottom and place on a plate, or place open-side up and finish with fish roe, if you like. Serve with the sushi ginger and wasabi.

SHISO TIP: shiso leaves may be easier to find, but you can also use shiso cress; you can stir all of the cress through the rice. Sushi fanatic Oof Verschuren (buy his book) told me this.

SUSHI VINEGAR TIP: you can buy ready-made sushi vinegar at the Asian grocery store or make it yourself. For the sushi vinegar, mix 40 ml (1¼ fl oz) of rice vinegar with 1½ tablespoons of granulated sugar and ½ teaspoon of salt. Keep stirring until the sugar and salt dissolve.

TOFU STUFFED WITH KETJAP

This recipe comes from Chinzy and Janet Choi, who call themselves the 'tofu girls' and who make the most delicious tofu in Rotterdam, under the name Choi Kee. If you visit the area, stop by their factory; they sell fresh tofu that, if you're lucky, is still warm. This recipe is another case of 'minimum effort, maximum result': you can buy fish paste, and the sauce is ready in a few minutes. The sisters were concerned that the recipe was too easy, and you could probably add a bunch of other ingredients, but sometimes simple is the best. The tofu girls serve the sauce alongside the tofu as a dip, but you can also toss the fried tofu in it.

SERVES: 3–4
PREP TIME: 20 MINUTES

FISH PASTE TIP: you can buy fish paste from the freezer section of any Asian grocery store. You can make it yourself, but it's hard to get it right and takes a lot of work.

500 g (1 lb 2 oz) firm tofu
150 g (5½ oz) fish paste
neutral oil, for frying
1 onion, chopped
2 tablespoons sambal oelek
60 ml (¼ cup) ketjap medja or manis
finely chopped coriander (cilantro), leaves
    and stems, to serve

Cut the tofu into 2 cm (¾ in) slices, and then into triangles. Use your knife to make a slit in the centre of the longest side to form an envelope, and fill the tofu with the fish paste.

Heat a generous layer of oil in a wok or frying pan over high heat and fry the tofu (in batches, if needed) for about 6 minutes, turning regularly, until the outside is golden brown and crispy. Remove the tofu from the pan and drain on a wire rack or paper towel. Drain the oil from the pan, leaving a few tablespoons.

Fry the onion for about 3 minutes over medium heat. Add the sambal and ketjap, mix well and let simmer for 1 minute. Remove from the heat and add in the coriander. Transfer the sauce to a bowl and serve alongside the tofu for dipping.

3

SAUCY

MAPO TOFU

There are already recipes for mapo tofu in my previous books, but you just can't make a tofu book without it. This is the dish that made me, and many of my friends, love tofu. That's probably the case for a lot of people, because mapo tofu is one of the most famous dishes from Sichuan. Silken tofu is prepared in a spicy, thick sauce made with Sichuan chilli bean paste and fermented black beans, which is also delicious on congee (see page 37), on a grilled cheese sandwich or with noodles. And yes, I know eight tablespoons of chilli bean paste is a lot, especially when combined with the optional chilli oil and powder, but I like it really spicy. Many recipes use two or three tablespoons, which you can start with.

SERVES: 4–6
PREP TIME: 20 MINUTES

MAKE IT VEGAN: replace the pork with 200 g (7 oz) of shiitake mushrooms, finely chopped into 2–5 mm (⅛–¼ in) pieces. Shiitake mushrooms require more oil and a little more time (8–10 minutes).

neutral oil, for frying
1 tablespoon crispy chilli oil (optional; see page 175)
150 g (5½ oz) minced (ground) pork
1–2 teaspoon chilli powder (optional)
3 tablespoons fermented black beans
4 garlic cloves, finely chopped
6 cm (2½ in) piece of ginger, finely chopped
4 spring onions (scallions), sliced into rings
120 g (4½ oz) Sichuan chilli bean paste
200 ml (7 fl oz) homemade stock (see pages 162–165) or water
600 g (1 lb 5 oz) silken tofu, cut into 2 cm (¾ in) cubes
1 tablespoon Sichuan peppercorns
steamed short-grained rice (see page 153), to serve (optional)
EQUIPMENT
mortar and pestle or spice/coffee grinder

Heat about 1 tablespoon of neutral oil and the chilli oil (if using) in a wok or frying pan over medium heat. Fry the minced pork for about 6 minutes, until the smallest pieces are browned and crispy. Add the chilli powder after 4 minutes, if using, and fry. Remove the mince from the pan and set aside while you make the sauce.

Briefly rinse the fermented beans. Heat another 1–2 tablespoons of oil in the same pan and fry the beans, garlic, ginger and white part of the spring onion for 1–2 minutes, until fragrant. Add the chilli bean paste and fry for a further 1 minute.

Return the minced meat to the pan, and add the stock or water. Add the tofu and carefully toss so that all the pieces are covered with sauce, then let simmer for about 1 minute, until the tofu is warm.

Grind the Sichuan peppecorns in a mortar or gringer and sprinkle over the mapo tofu. Do this with a sieve if necessary, so that you don't end up with large pieces of pepper between your teeth, although that is part of the experience. Sprinkle the green part of the spring onion over the tofu and serve with rice, if desired.

SILKEN TOFU WITH CORIANDER SAUCE

I'm a big proponent of good-on-everything sauces. Especially because, if all goes well, they make you get a little creative in the kitchen. Add a bit of cooking water for a nice noodle sauce, serve on labneh with pita for dipping, or add a small scoop to soy sauce to dip your dumplings into. This go-anywhere sauce has lots of coriander (cilantro), which works well on tofu, but I also like to eat it the next day on a cracker with cream cheese and tomato. If you keep leftovers on the counter, or at least in sight in the fridge, you will get inventive and come up with the best combinations. For this recipe, you steam the tofu so that it becomes warm and slightly firmer, but the sauce is just as tasty on cold silken tofu.

SERVES: 2
PREP TIME: 15 MINUTES

30 g (1 oz) coriander (cilantro), roughly
    chopped
1 garlic clove, roughly chopped
50 ml (1¾ fl oz) neutral oil
2 teaspoons chilli flakes
¼ teaspoon granulated sugar
¼ teaspoon MSG
1 tablespoon black vinegar
white pepper
1 teaspoon toasted sesame seeds
300 g (10½ oz) silken tofu, cut into 2 cm
    (¾ in) slices
peanuts in crispy chilli from Lao Gan Ma
    or chilli crisp of your choice, to serve

EQUIPMENT
hand blender or food processor
steamer or basket

With a hand blender or in a food processor, puree the coriander and garlic together with the oil, chilli flakes, sugar, MSG, black vinegar, a pinch of white pepper and a pinch of salt. Stir in the toasted sesame seeds last.

Bring water to the boil in a steamer or a saucepan with a steamer basket. Place the tofu on a plate that fits in your steamer or basket, and steam the tofu for 6 minutes. Remove from the steam and spoon the prepared coriander sauce and peanuts or chilli crisp on top.

DAN DAN NOODLES WITH TOFU

When you order dan dan noodles, you never know exactly what you will get. The noodles originated in Sichuan but are now popular across almost all of China (and the whole world), and every region has its own version. The dish's foundation is chilli oil and a creamy sauce made with sesame paste, but the proportions can vary quite a bit. In Chengdu, the noodles are dry (served without broth) and very spicy due to a good amount of chilli oil. In other places, the noodles come in broth, or the flavour of the sesame sauce is more dominant, or peanuts are used instead of sesame. In fact, some dan dan noodles are not spicy at all. These are.

SERVES: 2
PREP TIME: 20 MINUTES

neutral oil, for frying
1 garlic clove, finely chopped
1 cm (½ in) piece of ginger, finely chopped
1 tablespoon pickled mustard leaf, finely chopped
2 spring onions (scallions), thinly sliced into rings
¼ teaspoon chilli powder (optional)
150 g (5½ oz) firm tofu, crumbled
1 tablespoon Shaoxing rice wine
1 tablespoon dark soy sauce
¼ teaspoon MSG
200 g (7 oz) wheat noodles
2 tablespoons Peanut and/or Soy crispies (see pages 172 and 173)

Sauce
½ teaspoon Sichuan peppercorns
1 garlic clove, grated
60 g (¼ cup) Chinese sesame paste or tahini (see tip)
60 ml (¼ cup) crispy chilli oil (see page 175)
2 tablespoons light soy sauce
2 tablespoons black vinegar

EQUIPMENT
mortar and pestle

Heat a few tablespoons of oil in a wok or frying pan over medium–low heat and fry the garlic, ginger, mustard leaf and white part of the spring onion for 1–2 minutes, until fragrant. Add the chilli powder, if using, and cook for 30–60 seconds, until fragrant.

Add the tofu and fry for about 5 minutes, until most of the liquid that comes out of the tofu has evaporated. Add the Shaoxing rice wine and dark soy sauce and cook for 1–2 minutes, stirring constantly, until most of the liquid has evaporated. Add the MSG, taste, and season with salt.

For the sauce, crush the Sichuan peppercorns in a mortar. Add to a bowl with the rest of the ingredients and stir.

Bring a large pan of salted water to the boil and prepare the wheat noodles as directed on the package. Divide the sauce between two bowls, followed by the noodles and tofu. Place the green part of the spring onion and peanut and/or soy crispies on top, and serve. Stir the dish just before you start eating.

SESAME TIP: sesame paste and tahini vary greatly in taste by brand. So properly taste the sauce; you may need to add a little less sesame paste or an extra splash of cooking water.

'TOFU-BRAINS' WITH SPICY SAUCE

This silky tofu dish is commonly eaten in Sichuan and Tianjin. Doufu nao (the Sichuanese name) means 'tofu brain'. It may not sound very sexy, but it is. You first make a thick paste with cornflour (corn starch) and water, then crumble the tofu through it. Apparently that looks like a brain. You then spoon the mixture into a spicy sauce that you can make in a few minutes, creating a spicy tofu sauce. It's crazy with rice. You can also make the sauce and spoon it over (cold or warm) tofu pudding.

SERVES: 2
PREP TIME: 10 MINUTES

CRISPY TIP: I always prefer to have different types of crispies at home, but the reality is sometimes different. For those moments, I always have a bag of bhujia at home: a kind of Indian chips made from bean flour. My idol Fuchsia Dunlop often uses Bombay mix, also very tasty. Indian grocery stores/aisles have many more of these types of crispies, so do your research.

1 garlic clove, grated

2 tablespoons pickled mustard leaf, finely chopped

1 teaspoon grated ginger

2 tablespoons finely chopped coriander (cilantro)

2 tablespoons crispy chilli oil (see page 175) or use Lao Gan Ma

2 tablespoons soy sauce

1 teaspoon granulated sugar

1 tablespoon cornflour (corn starch)

300 g (10½ oz) silken tofu

1 spring onion (scallion), finely sliced into rings

bhujia (see tip) or Peanut crispies (see page 172), to serve

Place the garlic, mustard leaf, ginger, coriander, chilli oil, soy sauce and sugar in a large bowl and mix. If you want to make individual portions, you can also divide the sauce between two bowls.

Place the cornflour and 200 ml (7 fl oz) of water in a saucepan and bring to the boil. Reduce the heat and simmer gently until it thickens. Add the tofu to the pan and break into pieces with a fork. Stir well, turn off the heat and scoop the mixture into the bowl(s) on top of the sauce. Sprinkle the spring onion over the tofu.

Toss the tofu and sauce together when you're at the table and serve the crispies on the side. They can also go on top, but then they get soggy. I like to sprinkle some each time I take a bite (just like parmesan cheese when I eat pasta).

KOREAN TOFU STEW WITH CLAMS

Jiigae is a spicy Korean stew that's served in an earthenware pot, so that it still bubbles wonderfully on the table. Basically you can make it with anything: kimchi, pork belly, vegetables, seafood and of course tofu. I'm always looking for an excuse to eat clams, so I added those here. And a few prawns (shrimp) and dried anchovies. Everything is allowed. Mussels would be nice too, I think. For this dish I always use silken tofu, which is sometimes sold as a cylinder (similar to egg tofu). This stew is also delicious with Homemade tofu (see page 23), if you have any leftovers.

SERVES: 4
PREP TIME: 35 MINUTES
WAITING TIME: 1 HOUR

400 g (14 oz) clams or cockles
6 dried anchovies (see tip)
15 g (½ oz) kombu
neutral oil, for frying
1 small onion, chopped
1 garlic clove, finely chopped
2 tablespoons gochugaru
2 tablespoons sesame oil
1 tablespoon Korean or light soy sauce
500 g (1 lb 2 oz) silken tofu, broken into
    large chunks
5 prawns (shrimp), peeled and deveined
100 g (3½ oz) enoki mushrooms
1 egg
1 spring onion (scallion), finely chopped

Put a few tablespoons of salt in a bowl of cold water and stir until the salt dissolves. Put the clams or cockles in the salt water and leave for 20 minutes to 1 hour. All the sand should settle to the bottom of the bowl. Remove the shells from the water and rinse in a sieve.

Meanwhile, place the anchovies and kombu in a saucepan with 750 ml (3 cups) of water and bring to the boil. Put the lid on the pan, reduce the heat and simmer gently for 20 minutes. Strain the stock into a bowl and set aside.

Heat a few tablespoons of oil in a thick-bottomed earthenware pot or frying pan over medium–low heat and fry the onion and garlic for about 3 minutes, until fragrant. Add the gochugaru and sesame oil and fry for 30 seconds. Add the strained stock and soy sauce, and bring to the boil. Taste and season with salt.

Reduce the heat to medium–low and add the tofu, prawns and clams to the pot with the stock and place the enoki on top. Cover the pot and simmer for 3 minutes, until the shells have opened. Break the egg into the centre, and cook for a further 1 minute, until the egg whites have set. Sprinkle the spring onion over the stew and serve.

MAKE IT VEGETARIAN: leave out the anchovies, clams and prawns. Add extra mushrooms or some kimchi, if desired.

ANCHOVY TIP: you can buy different types of dried anchovies; pick nice large ones to make stock with. Small anchovies will also work, just use a little more.

PAN TIP: if you have an earthenware pot (clay pot or donabe-style pot), use that. They retain the heat well when you put them on the table. If not, use a frying pan or, if necessary, a wok.

SAUCY

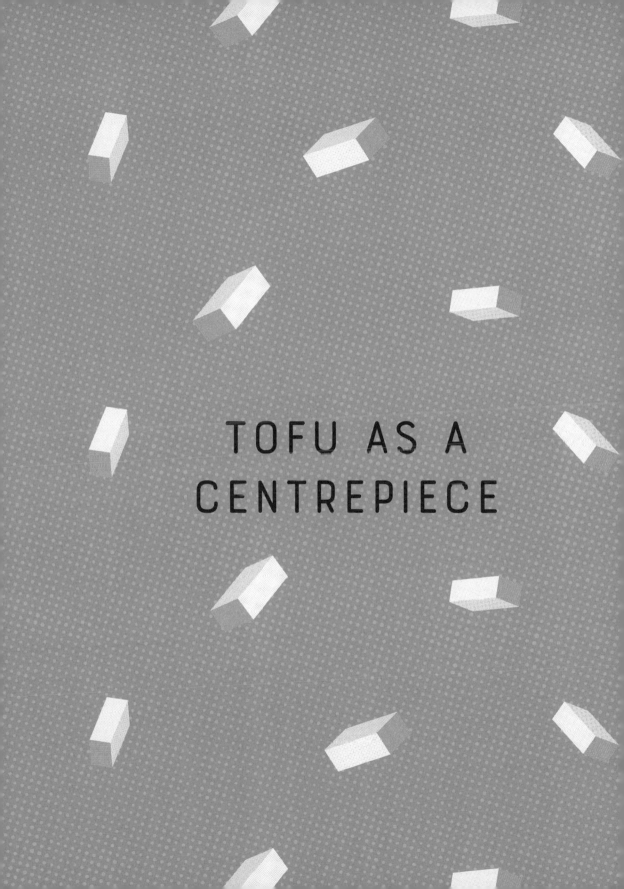

TOFU AS A
CENTREPIECE

TOFU AS A CENTREPIECE

I'd like to advocate for tofu as a centrepiece. I really don't want to be one of those people who make a chickpea burger and claim it tastes just as good as beef, but tofu as a showpiece is fantastic. In Singapore, I often ate tofu that was deep-fried in its entirety, which looks very impressive. Leave it whole or cut it into slices after frying, because the contrast of the fried exterior and the snow-white interior is beautiful. By deep-frying the tofu at a high temperature, its exterior comes loose, and you get a very nice fried layer around the tofu. I prefer to use soft tofu for deep-frying, which is sold in nice big blocks that are wonderfully soft inside. If you're a little more down to earth or it's a weekday, all the sauces in this chapter are also delicious on small cubes of fried tofu.

Whole fried tofu recipe:

Heat neutral oil in a wok or deep-fryer to 200°C (400°F), or until a cube of bread dropped in the oil browns in 5 seconds. Due to the high temperature, the outside of the tofu separates from the rest and a new layer is created – you want that to happen. Fry a block of soft tofu (500 g/1 lb 2 oz) for about 10 minutes. Make sure that the tofu does not touch the bottom of the pan; to prevent this, slide a spatula under the tofu to raise it slightly. If there isn't enough oil in the pan to cover the tofu, you can drizzle the hot oil over the top of the tofu. Or turn the tofu halfway through, but be careful. Remove the tofu from the pan and drain on a wire rack or paper towel.

DEEP-FRIED TOFU WITH GARLIC SAUCE

My first experience in Singapore with tofu fried whole was in my hotel room while I was awaiting the results of my PCR test and at the mercy of delivery apps. I ordered Hainanese chicken rice, the national dish of Singapore, from Tiong Bahru Chicken Rice and saw 'special tofu' on the menu. Of course that had to be in my basket. The fried tofu came in a syrupy sauce with lots and lots of garlic. Luckily no one was allowed near me. For this recipe, you make garlic crispies. With the left-over garlic oil, you make the sauce for the tofu, to which you also add fresh garlic. Heavenly.

SERVES: 2–3
PREP TIME: 20 MINUTES

500 g (1 lb 2 oz) soft tofu
neutral oil, for frying
3 garlic cloves, finely chopped
1 red chilli
2 tablespoons oyster sauce
   or mushroom sauce
1 tablespoon light soy sauce
½ teaspoon granulated sugar
1 teaspoon cornflour (corn starch)

Fry the tofu according to the instructions on page 101. Set aside.

Set up a sieve over a heatproof bowl. Heat 60 ml (¼ cup) of oil in a wok or frying pan over low heat and fry two-thirds of the garlic for about 5 minutes, until golden brown and crispy. Watch out: the crispies will burn quickly at the end, so take them out of the pan in time. Strain the garlic over a bowl and save the oil.

Cut a few rings from the chilli and set aside for garnish. Finely chop the rest of the chilli (or a little less, if you don't like spice). Heat the garlic oil in the wok or frying pan over medium heat and fry the chilli and the rest of the garlic for 1–2 minutes, until softened and fragrant.

Meanwhile, mix the oyster sauce or mushroom sauce with the soy sauce, sugar, cornflour and 2 tablespoons of water in a small bowl. Add to the pan and simmer gently for 1–2 minutes, until the sauce thickens. Add the tofu to the pan, carefully turn in the sauce and let simmer for about 1 minute on each side, so that the tofu absorbs some of the sauce.

Put the tofu on a plate to serve and garnish with the garlic crispies and chilli.

DEEP-FRIED TOFU WITH TURMERIC CARAMEL

This spectacular tofu is inspired by the Vietnamese dish, cha ca la vong, which features fried fish in a sauce with a good amount of turmeric and dill. Dill is one of my favourite herbs, but it's not found in many Asian kitchens, so when I get the chance to use it, I grab with both hands. Vietnamese cuisine also uses a lot of caramel sauce, which is beautiful and golden yellow in this dish. When you cut the tofu, the yellow caramel seeps through the white tofu a bit. It becomes almost marble-like, which greatly adds to the wow factor.

SERVES: 2–3
PREP TIME: 20 MINUTES

3 garlic cloves
100 g (3½ oz) light brown sugar
100 ml (3½ fl oz) rice vinegar
2 teaspoons ground turmeric
500 g (1 lb 2 oz) soft tofu
neutral oil, for frying
lots of dill leaves, to serve
salt flakes, to serve (optional)

Crush the garlic with the side of your knife and place in a saucepan with the sugar, rice vinegar and turmeric. Bring to the boil, then reduce the heat to medium low and simmer for 2–3 minutes until the sauce thickens slightly, adjusting the heat as needed. Turn off the heat and let the sauce cool. As it does, it will thicken a bit.

Fry the tofu according to the instructions on page 101. Carefully dip the tofu into the turmeric caramel, place on a plate and serve with the dill on top and a pinch of salt flakes, if desired.

DEEP-FRIED SEAWEED TOFU WITH CRAB SAUCE

I ate this dish in Singapore at Jumbo Seafood, a restaurant known for its perfectly executed chilli crab. The tofu we ordered came in an insane crab sauce, but the most amazing thing about this dish was the seaweed they stuck to the tofu before it went into the fryer. Of course it was very tasty, but this chapter's focus is on presentation, which is completely upgraded by that fantastic trick. If you find it complicated to fold the nori around the tofu, you can also just stick a layer on top. That's how they served it at Jumbo, but I alway want more nori, personally. For the presentation's finishing touch, we go all out and circle the dish with broccoli florets.

SERVES: 2–3
PREP TIME: 30 MINUTES

250 g (9 oz) broccoli florets (see tip)
neutral oil, for frying
100 g (3½ oz) shiitake mushrooms, cubed
125 g (4½ oz) crabmeat
200 ml (7 fl oz) homemade stock
    (see pages 162–165)
1 tablespoon Shaoxing rice wine
1 teaspoon cornflour (corn starch), mixed
    with 2 tablespoons of cold water
2 nori sheets
500 g (1 lb 2 oz) soft tofu

EQUIPMENT
kitchen thermometer (optional)

Bring a large pot of salted water to the boil and cook the broccoli florets for 2 minutes. Allow to drain and set aside.

Heat a few tablespoons of oil in a wok or frying pan over high heat and fry the shiitake mushrooms for about 5 minutes, until tender. Add the crabmeat along with the stock and Shaoxing and bring to the boil. Add the cornflour and allow the sauce to simmer until it thickens slightly. Turn off the heat and set aside.

Fold the nori around the block of tofu. If necessary, cut the nori into pieces so this is easier; it's not a problem if the nori cracks a bit. Push the nori firmly against the tofu so that it moistens and softens. This will help the nori stick to the tofu so everything fries in one piece.

Heat a generous layer of oil in a wok or frying pan to 180°C (350°F) or until a cube of bread dropped in the oil browns in 15 seconds. Fry the tofu for about 3–5 minutes, until golden brown and crispy. Drain the tofu on a wire rack. Warm the sauce slightly and stir in the broccoli. Place the tofu on a plate and circle with the broccoli. Spoon the sauce over the tofu and serve.

MAKE IT VEGAN: use vegan stock and omit the crab (add a little more mushroom).

BROCCOLI TIP: normally I'm a big fan of cooking the broccoli stalk, but here we're going for presentation. Slices of stalk aren't so pretty. You can cut it very thinly with a mandoline or vegetable peeler and serve it as a snack with some lime juice, fish sauce and a pinch of light brown sugar.

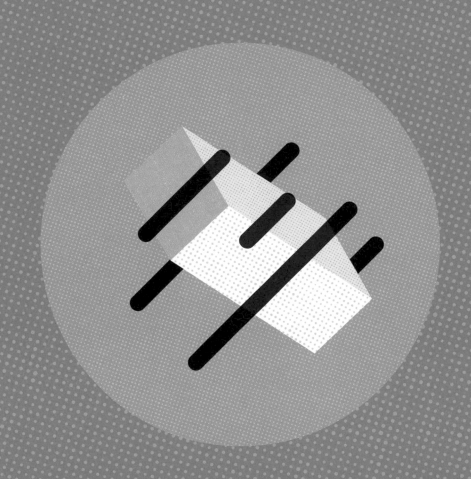

4

NOT SO
SAUCY

CRACK TOFU

This dish originated when I found myself with little cognitive capacity after the launch of my second book (I always call this period my after-book burnout), but with a lot of tofu in the fridge. In total tofu panic, I turned to my friend Marieke, who very casually told me that she had coated tofu the day before in cornflour (corn starch), pepper and MSG. Add black beans to the pan and that's it. Sounds simple, but I found tofu coated in MSG quite brilliant.

Normally I rinse fermented black beans to soften their flavour, but I quickly decided that this would be the ultimate salty/umami tofu. Do not rinse the beans, use salty peanuts and finish the dish with crispy chilli from Lao Gan Ma, which also has a lot of MSG in it. Due to the aforementioned mini burnout, I accidentally threw spring onion (scallion) – which I had wanted to keep as a fresh topping – in the pan at the same time as the beans and peanuts. A blessing in disguise, because briefly frying the spring onion gives it a roasted taste that comes damn close to umami.

SERVES: 1–2
PREP TIME: 20 MINUTES

30 g (1 oz) cornflour (corn starch)
¼ teaspoon MSG
½ teaspoon white pepper
¼ teaspoon salt
250 g (9 oz) firm tofu, cut into 3 cm (1¼ in) cubes
neutral oil, for frying
1 tablespoon fermented black beans, coarsley chopped
2 tablespoons salted peanuts, coarsley chopped
1 spring onion (scallion), thinly sliced into rings
crispy chilli from Lao Gan Ma, to serve

Mix the cornflour in a bowl with the MSG, white pepper and salt. Add the tofu and toss to coat all sides.

Heat a generous layer of oil in a wok or frying pan over high heat and fry the tofu on all sides for 8–10 minutes in total, until golden brown and crispy.

Drain the oil from the pan, leaving 1–2 tablespoons. Add the black beans, peanuts and spring onion to the pan and cook over medium heat for 2–3 minutes (be careful not to burn the peanuts), until the spring onion is just beginning to brown. Remove the tofu from the pan and serve with crispy chilli.

STICKY KOREAN TOFU

In plenty of Asian countries, tourist restaurants serve a version of sweet and sour chicken, which is usually far too sweet. But not in Korea, where you can get kkanpunggi: crispy fried chicken served in a perfectly balanced sweet and sour sauce. That sauce is also very tasty with crispy tofu. Bell pepper (capsicum) is often added, but I don't like when vegetables find their way into my tofu; I prefer to make a separate vegetable dish, like a salad with my Korean dressing (see page 158).

I copied Korean YouTube queen Maangchi's technique of preparing a spring onion (scallion) and garlic chilli oil first, which I then use to make a sauce. This method makes the sauce taste slightly roasted, and you end up with spring onion and garlic crispies. Of course, I would never say no to that.

SERVES: 2
PREP TIME: 20 MINUTES

4 spring onions (scallions)
100 ml (3½ fl oz) neutral oil + extra
  for frying
2 garlic cloves, very finely sliced
1½ tablespoons granulated sugar
1 teaspoon cornflour (corn starch) + extra
  for coating
2 tablespoons Korean or light soy sauce
1½ tablespoons rice vinegar
2 tablespoons gochugaru
250 g (9 oz) firm tofu, cut into 1 cm
  (½ in) cubes
3 cm (1¼ in) piece of ginger, thinly sliced
1 red chilli, sliced into rings

Slice the spring onions into 5 cm (2 in) pieces, then cut them into thin strips. This is not fun work; if you feel lazy, you can slice the spring onion into thin rings.

Heat the oil in a wok or frying pan over medium heat and fry the spring onion and garlic for 8 10 minutes, until golden brown and crispy. The oil should simmer gently the entire time. If it's bubbling too much, reduce the heat a bit.

Meanwhile, mix the sugar, cornflour, soy sauce, rice vinegar and 2 tablespoons of water in a small bowl to make the sauce.

Place the gochugaru in a heatproof bowl and place a fine sieve over it. Drain the spring onion and garlic over the bowl of gochugaru so that it sizzles. Stir the oil so that the gochugaru is evenly distributed and set aside while you prepare the rest of the ingredients. Let the spring onion and garlic drain slightly on a paper towel-lined plate.

See next page

Coat the tofu in 2 tablespoons of cornflour. Heat a generous layer of oil in a wok or frying pan over medium heat and fry the tofu for 8–10 minutes, until golden brown and crispy. Remove from the pan and drain on a wire rack or paper towel. Drain the oil from the pan and wipe clean.

Strain the gochugaru from the reserved oil. Heat the oil in the wok or frying pan over medium heat, and fry the ginger and chilli for 1 minute. Add the tofu and sauce and cook for a further 1–2 minutes, until the sauce has reduced slightly and sticks to the tofu.

Turn off the heat and stir three-quarters of the spring onion and garlic crispies into the tofu. Transfer to a plate or bowl and place the remaining crispies on top.

PAD KRAPOW WITH TOFU

One of my favourite dishes in Thailand is pad krapow: greasy minced (ground) meat with holy basil and a fried egg on top. It has just enough sauce to give the mince a lot of flavour without making things too saucy. Crunchy is *key* here. Because you bake the crumbled tofu until it's super crispy first, then add the sauce, you get the perfect texture (crispy outside, juicy inside).

For this dish, you need holy basil: this is not the same as Thai basil. Holy basil is sweet and peppery, and Thai basil tastes of aniseed. If you can't find holy, you can use Thai. Use a little less, otherwise its flavour can dominate. Just make sure to serve your pad krapow with a greasy and crispy egg, which completes the dish.

SERVES: 2
PREP TIME: 20 MINUTES

MAKE IT VEGETARIAN: replace the oyster sauce with mushroom sauce.

250 g (9 oz) firm tofu
25 g (1 oz) cornflour (corn starch)
neutral oil, for frying
2 garlic cloves, finely chopped
1 red chilli, finely chopped
2 tablespoons light soy sauce
2 tablespoons oyster sauce or
    mushroom sauce
40 holy or Thai basil leaves
2 eggs
steamed jasmine rice (see page 153), to
    serve

Crumble the tofu until some is almost crumbs and the rest is slightly larger; this way, you end up with the perfect marriage of crispy and juicy. Mix the tofu with the cornflour.

Heat a generous layer of oil in a wok or frying pan over high heat and fry the tofu for 10 minutes, until golden brown and crispy. The tofu should be really crispy: when you think it's done, fry it a little longer just to be sure. The cornflour can make the tofu rather sticky, so separate the tofu with a silicone spatula or slotted spoon. When the tofu is done, remove it with a slotted spoon or drain it in a sieve over a heatproof bowl.

Drain the oil from the pan, leaving about 2 tablespoons. Saute the garlic and chilli for about 1 minute over medium heat. Add the tofu, soy sauce and oyster or mushroom sauce to the pan and toss. Fry for about 1 further minute, until the sauce has been absorbed by the tofu. Turn off the heat, add the basil and stir until it wilts.

Transfer the tofu to a plate or bowl and wipe the pan clean. Fry the eggs as instructed on page 158. Serve the pad krapow on a bowl of jasmine rice with a crispy egg on top.

NASI LEMAK WITH DOUBLE TOFU

I will never understand how so many Dutch people prefer to have breakfast with a bowl of yoghurt, rather than fragrant coconut rice. I think I feel so at home in Asia because I'm not the only one there who enjoys rice with crispies in the morning. Nasi lemak – coconut rice with sambal, peanuts, anchovies, egg and sometimes extra dressing – is a typical breakfast dish in Malaysia, Singapore and Indonesia, and it's my favourite when I visit.

I go wild with the peanuts and anchovies when I make the crispies, which are gooey, sweet and spicy. For extra crunch, I add fried tofu and shallots. Welcome to sticky, crispy heaven. You will make more crispies than you need, but they also work very well as chips. It is important that the rice is not too oily, so buy coconut milk with the fat solidified on top (Kara, for example) and use the coconut water underneath to cook the rice. Use the rest of the tin to marinate the tofu.

SERVES: 2
PREP TIME: 1 HOUR

Turmeric tofu
250 g (9 oz) firm tofu
250 ml (1 cup) coconut milk
8 lime leaves, crushed
1 teaspoon ground turmeric
1 teaspoon salt
neutral oil, for frying

Coconut rice
200 g (7 oz) jasmine rice, rinsed until the
    water runs clear
150 ml (5 fl oz) coconut milk
    (see recipe intro)
4 pandan leaves

Sticky crispies
20 tofu skin sheets
boiling water
neutral oil, for frying
25 g (1 oz) dried anchovies (see tip)
50 g (1¾ oz) unsalted peanuts

Cut the tofu into 1.5 cm (½ in) slices, then into triangles.

For the turmeric tofu, skim the fat from the top of the coconut milk and place in a saucepan. Set aside 150 ml (5 fl oz) of the coconut milk for the rice and pour the rest into the pan with the fat. Add the lime leaves, turmeric, salt and tofu. Bring to the boil, reduce the heat to low and simmer gently for 5 minutes. Turn off the heat and let the tofu cool in the coconut milk. You can also do this in advance; the tofu will keep for a day or two in the fridge, and will continue to absorb the flavours.

For the coconut rice, place the rice in a saucepan with 150 ml (5 fl oz) of water. Pour the reserved coconut milk into the pan and add a pinch of salt. Tie a knot in the pandan leaves and add to the pan. Bring the rice to the boil and cover. Set the heat to the lowest setting and cook the rice for 12–15 minutes, until the water has evaporated. Turn off the heat and set aside while you prepare the rest of the ingredients.

To make the crispies, break the tofu skin sheets into pieces in a bowl and pour over boiling water. Let sit for a few minutes, until the sheets are soft.

Heat a generous layer of oil in a wok or frying pan over medium heat and fry the anchovies for about 2 minutes, until golden brown and crispy. Remove from the oil and drain on paper towel.

1 shallot, thinly sliced into rings
3 tablespoons granulated sugar
3 tablespoons sambal (see tip)

To garnish
¼ long cucumber, sliced
2 hard-boiled eggs, peeled and halved
sambal

Fry the peanuts in the same oil for about 2 minutes, until a few shades darker. Remove from the pan and drain on paper towel.

Fry the shallot (also in the same oil) for about 2 minutes, until softened and darkened (it doesn't have to be very crispy). Scoop it out of the pan and set aside.

Drain the tofu skins and pat dry. Fry for 2–3 minutes until crispy, and drain on paper towel.

Drain the oil from the pan and wipe it clean. Heat the sugar in the same pan over medium heat, until it melts and turns light brown. Add the sambal and stir together. Add the anchovies, peanuts, shallot and tofu skins, and toss until everything is covered in a thin layer of sticky sweetness. Remove from the pan and set aside.

Wash the pan and heat a good layer of fresh oil in it. Remove the tofu from the coconut milk and pat dry with paper towel. Fry the tofu over medium heat for about 4 minutes, until lightly browned. Remove from the oil and drain.

Put half the rice in a bowl and press down. Invert the bowl onto a plate and hit the bottom gently so that the rice comes out as a mould. Repeat for the second plate.

Divide the tofu, cucumber, eggs and sticky crispies over the plates. Serve with another scoop of sambal

MAKE IT VEGETARIAN: you can omit the anchovies for a vegetarian version.

ANCHOVY TIP: you can buy different types of dried anchovies. Pick small ones since they fry the best. Large ones are better for making stock.

SAMBAL TIP: with nasi lemak, it is important that you use really good sambal. Mine has a lot of lime leaf, so see if you can find something similar.

FRIED COCONUT RICE

Have left-over coconut rice from Nasi lemak (see page 120)? Please make fried coconut rice. Because of the fat from the coconut milk that the rice was cooked in, the rice fries perfectly without sticking. Add a pinch of salt and MSG, and you're done. This seems simple, but it is really mind-blowing. Fried egg, sambal and fried onions are tasty on top, but the rice is also delicious enough to eat on its own.

SERVES: 1
PREP TIME: 10 MINUTES

left-over coconut rice (see page 120)
neutral oil, for frying
pinch of MSG
left-over turmeric tofu (optional, if you
    happen to have leftovers), cubed
1 Crispy egg (see page 158)
good-quality sambal, to serve
fried onions (available at Asian
    grocery stores), to serve

Loosen the rice with a fork. Heat a few tablespoons of oil in a wok or frying pan over high heat. Add the rice to the pan with the MSG and a pinch of salt, stir and press into the pan. Fry for about 1 minute, then stir. Fry for another 1–2 minutes, until the rice is starting to brown. Spoon the tofu through the rice (if using) and warm it up briefly. Serve with the crispy egg, sambal and fried onions.

SICHUAN BARBECUE TOFU

When I was in Mandarin class, I was looking for a language buddy to practise with, when I stumbled upon Xinyu Zhu. She is from Chengdu and has been living in Rotterdam for years, where she teaches Chinese cooking workshops. Coincidentally, she also sells the most delicious Sichuan peppercorns. We spoke on Zoom for months, where she never understood me because of my lousy pronunciation, but taught me how to say that I write cookbooks and that I really like tofu. This is her recipe. It is a dish she often ate at a street stall near her grandmother's house. When the stall was closed one day, her grandmother made the dish for her, so it always reminds Xinyu of her grandmother and her hometown.

SERVES: 3–4
PREP TIME: 35 MINUTES

2 star anise
3 bay leaves
400 g (14 oz) firm tofu
neutral oil, for frying
2 garlic cloves, thinly sliced
15 g (½ oz) ginger, thinly sliced
5 g (¼ oz) Sichuan dried chillies
¼ teaspoon green Sichuan peppercorns
1 tablespoon Sichuan chilli bean paste
½ teaspoon granulated sugar
1 teaspoon normal (all-purpose) or light
    soy sauce (see tip)
1 teaspoon chicken stock powder or
    mushroom powder
6 spring onions (scallions), sliced into
    3 cm (1¼ in) pieces
1 teaspoon ground cumin
1 teaspoon dark soy sauce
½ teaspoon green Sichuan peppercorn oil
    (see page 157) or use store-bought

Soak the star anise and bay leaves in 2 tablespoons of water while you prepare the rest of the ingredients.

Slice the tofu in half lengthways and then into 1–2 cm (½–¾ in) pieces. Place the tofu on a plate and sprinkle with a little salt, then let sit for 3 minutes.

Meanwhile, heat a few tablespoons of oil in a wok or frying pan over medium heat. When the tofu is ready, fry it in a single layer for about 5 minutes on both sides, until golden brown. Remove the tofu from the pan and drain on paper towel.

If necessary, add a little more oil to the pan. Fry the garlic and ginger for about 1 minute. Add the dried chillies, peppercorns and chilli bean paste. Cook until fragrant, about 3 minutes. Add the tofu and stir-fry until all of it is coated in sauce. Add the sugar, soy sauce and stock powder, and stir. Remove the star anise and bay leaves from the water, and add the water to the pan. Let simmer for about 1 minute.

Turn the heat up to high and add the spring onion, cumin, dark soy sauce and peppercorn oil, and stir-fry for another 20 seconds. Turn off the heat, transfer to a platter and serve.

MAKE IT VEGAN: replace the chicken stock powder with mushroom powder. You can easily make this yourself by grinding dried shiitake mushrooms in a blender or spice/coffee grinder. Strain through a sieve to remove the large chunks. Stays good for a while and is a real umami bomb.

SOY SAUCE TIP: this recipe uses 'normal' (all-purpose) soy sauce. This is widely used in Sichuan cuisine. The taste is slightly saltier, stronger and more intense than light soy sauce, with a very pure soy taste. Xinyu recommends the Wan Ja Shan brand (with an orange label). If you don't have it, you can also use light soy sauce, but the dish will taste slightly different.

CHONGQING TOFU

Chongqing chicken is a famous Sichuan dish (the city of Chongqing used to be in the Chinese province of Sichuan), in which fried chicken is buried under a huge pile of dried chillies. You fish the chicken out of the chillies with skewers, digging out larger tender pieces and super crispy smaller bites. For the perfect juicy-crispy ratio, break the tofu into two different sizes. If you don't like spice, this dish may not be for you. If you still want to give it a try, reduce the amount of chilli powder, rather than the dried chilli. The dried chilli provides more chilli aroma. The powder provides pure zing.

SERVES: 3–4
PREP TIME: 30 MINUTES

1 teaspoon Sichuan peppercorns
¼ teaspoon cumin seeds
1 teaspoon chilli powder
pinch of MSG
500 g (1 lb 2 oz) firm tofu
neutral oil, for frying
60 g (2 oz) cornflour (corn starch)
1 garlic clove, finely chopped
1 cm (½ in) piece of ginger, finely chopped
1 spring onion (scallion), white part finely
    chopped, green part finely sliced
    into rings
20 dried chillies (preferably from
    Sichuan), seeded and chopped
    into 1.25 cm (½ in) pieces

EQUIPMENT
mortar and pestle or spice/coffee grinder

Toast the Sichuan peppercorns and cumin seeds in a dry wok or frying pan over medium heat for about 1 minute. Remove from the pan and grind in a mortar or grinder. Mix in the chilli powder, MSG and a pinch of salt.

Finely crumble 200 g (7 oz) of the tofu. Crumble 300 g (10½ oz) into coarser pieces, and put the tofu in two different bowls.

Heat a generous layer of oil in a wok or frying pan over high heat. Mix the finely crumbled tofu with 2 tablespoons of cornflour and fry for about 10 minutes, until golden brown and crispy. Remove from the pan and drain on paper towel. Mix the coarse tofu with the remaining cornflour and fry for 10 minutes, until it's also golden brown and crispy. If your pan is large enough, you can fry all of the tofu at once, but you probably won't be able to. Remove the tofu from the pan and set aside.

Wipe the pan clean and heat a few tablespoons of oil in it over medium heat. Fry the garlic, ginger and white part of the spring onion for about 1 minute, until fragrant. Add the dried chilli and cook for 30–60 seconds until lightly browned, being careful not to burn it. Add the tofu and spice mixture and stir. Turn off the heat and serve with the green part of the spring onion on top.

SPRING ONION TOFU

I was recently approached by someone who asked if I was 'that spring onion influencer'. The word influencer gives me an acute itch, but if I want to influence something, it's spring onion (scallion), so I started to glow a bit.

In this dish, besides tofu, there is not much more than spring onion. That may seem boring, but it isn't. I ate the same dish on a sweltering day in Singapore, where I wrote part of this book. For research, I almost always ordered a tofu dish, and this was on the menu as 'onion tofu'. I had no idea what that meant, of course, and it turned out to be little more than tofu with spring onion. But man, was I impressed. The soft texture of the tofu and the freshness of the spring onion (and I think a splash of vinegar) were exactly what I was craving.

It is extremely important for this dish that you get the right tofu (soft). Normally I instruct you to chop spring onions very finely, but in this dish, it's nice to really bite into larger pieces. Soak the spring onion in water for a while to take off the worst of the sharpness.

SERVES: 2–3
PREP TIME: 10 MINUTES

2 spring onions (scallions), sliced into
    5 mm (¼ in) pieces
500 g (1 lb 2 oz) soft tofu
2 teaspoons spring onion oil (left-over from
    the Spring onion crispies; see page 173)
    or use store-bought
2 teaspoons rice vinegar

Place the spring onion in a bowl of cold water for 5 minutes. Meanwhile, place the tofu in a bowl and mash with a fork; the tofu should be broken up, but there should still be large chunks.

Remove the spring onion from the water and add to the tofu. Add the spring onion oil, rice vinegar and a pinch of salt. Mix gently, taste and season with additional salt, if needed.

TOFU LARB

Larb is a dish commonly eaten in Laos and northern Thailand. It is often made of meat, but I sometimes make it with eggplant (aubergine) or – as I do here – with tofu. The fresh dressing with fish sauce, lime and herbs would probably make even a dry cracker tasty. I don't fry the tofu until it's crispy in this dish, because I like it when it stays a bit soft. It also saves a lot of oil and time, which is always nice. Larb is often served with steamed glutinous rice and lettuce leaves to eat it in. You have to soak glutinous rice in the morning and I always forget that, so my larb often ends up on top of a bowl of jasmine rice.

SERVES: 2–3
PREP TIME: 20 MINUTES

MAKE IT VEGAN: larb is traditionally made with fish sauce. To make this dish vegan, you can replace it with light soy sauce.

2 tablespoons glutinous rice
1 small shallot, thinly sliced into rings
neutral oil, for frying
300 g (10½ oz) firm tofu, crumbled
1 garlic clove, finely chopped
½ red chilli, finely chopped
juice of 1 lime
1 tablespoon fish sauce or light soy sauce
1 tablespoon light brown sugar
15 g (½ oz) coriander (cilantro), leaves and
    stems finely chopped
20 mint leaves, finely chopped
steamed rice (see page 153), to serve
    (optional)

EQUIPMENT
mortar and pestle or spice/coffee grinder

Heat a frying pan over medium heat and toast the rice in it for about 5 minutes, until golden brown. Watch out that the rice doesn't cook too quickly – if necessary, reduce the heat a bit. Let cool slightly and grind in a mortar or grinder.

Place the shallot in cold water. Heat a few tablespoons of oil in a wok or frying pan over high heat and fry the tofu for 3–5 minutes, until the moisture has evaporated and the tofu is beginning to brown. Add the garlic and chilli to the pan and fry for a further 1 minute.

Mix the lime juice, fish sauce or soy sauce and sugar in a bowl. Stir the dressing through the tofu, followed by the coriander and mint. Stir half of the glutinous rice powder and all of the shallot into the tofu. Sprinkle the other half of the rice powder over the dish, and serve over rice, if desired.

KOREAN FRIED TOFU WITH GINGER SOY GLAZE

Many people think of Korean fried chicken as yangnyeom: chicken in a fiery red sauce made with gochujang. It's delicious, but there's another version with a sweet and sticky, soy and sugar-based glaze that's just as delicious: dakgangjeong. I coat tofu with that sauce here, and a friend said that it was even better than the chicken. I use soft tofu for this recipe, which is very fragile. It may break a bit, but this does contribute to the perfectly soft-but-crunchy texture. Warm up the sauce before mixing the tofu in, and stir as gently as possible. As long as you do, there's nothing to worry about, and you can always use firm tofu.

SERVES: 3
PREP TIME: 30 MINUTES

Sauce
2 garlic cloves, grated
3 cm (1¼ in) piece of ginger, grated
2 tablespoons gochugaru
50 g (1¾ oz) dark brown sugar
60 ml (¼ cup) light soy sauce
1 tablespoon white vinegar
2 tablespoons toasted sesame seeds

Tofu
neutral oil, for frying
50 g (1¾ oz) cornflour (corn starch)
1 teaspoon salt
½ teaspoon garlic powder
½ teaspoon ground ginger
500 g (1 lb 2 oz) soft tofu, cubed

For the sauce, place the garlic and ginger in a saucepan with the gochugaru, sugar, soy sauce and vinegar. Bring to the boil, then reduce the heat and let the sauce simmer for 2 minutes. Set aside while you prepare the tofu.

Heat a generous layer of oil in a wok or frying pan over high heat.

Mix the cornflour with the salt, garlic powder and ground ginger. Carefully roll half of the tofu through the cornflour mixture; if you try with all the tofu at once, it will break more easily, and the cornflour will clump.

Fry the coated tofu for about 5 minutes, until light brown and crispy. Drain on a wire rack or paper towel, and repeat with the rest of the tofu.

Reheat the sauce slightly so that it becomes more liquid, add to a large bowl with the toasted sesame seeds and tofu, and toss gently. Place on a platter and serve.

TEA TOFU

I did not come up with this dish myself: it's directly from Ka Fai Lee (pappa Lee, for those who know him), the chef of Chinese–Indonesian restaurant Fook Sing in Amsterdam. I asked if he ever cooked with tea and this fantastic tofu recipe immediately popped out of his mouth. It is incredibly simple and very light on the palate. By using tea and tea powder, the tofu takes on a wonderfully subtle flavour. Use good-quality green tea; I used longjing (also called 'dragon well'), which is nice and grassy. If you don't have a grinder to make tea powder, you can also use store-bought matcha powder (see note on page 143).

SERVES: 2
PREP TIME: 20 MINUTES

2 teaspoons good-quality green tea leaves, ground (see recipe intro) + extra to make tea
neutral oil, for frying
250 g (9 oz) firm tofu, cubed
1 spring onion (scallion), finely sliced into rings

EQUIPMENT
spice/coffee grinder

Make a pot of green tea according to the package instructions. Save 200 ml (7 fl oz) for the tofu and drink the rest while cooking.

Heat a generous layer of oil in a wok or frying pan over high heat. Fry the tofu for about 10 minutes, until golden brown and crispy. Drain the oil from the pan, leaving 1–2 tablespoons. Add the spring onion and a pinch of salt, toss everything and fry for about 1 minute.

Add enough tea to cover the tofu halfway, the amount depends on the size of your pan, and can vary from 50–200 ml (1¾–7 fl oz). Let simmer for a few minutes, until the tea has mostly reduced. You only want a tiny bit of moisture in the pan.

Place the tofu on a plate, wet side down, and top with the spring onion and remaining sauce. Sprinkle the green tea powder over the tofu and serve.

5

SWEET

CHOCOLATE CUSTARD WITH SESAME TEA CRUMBLE

The biggest reason I like tofu is that good tofu has a custard-like texture. No wonder then that silken tofu is often used to make a delicious, creamy chocolate dessert. This dessert is often called chocolate mousse, but I think it looks more like firm custard. It has a very smooth texture, which is exactly what I like. I use dark chocolate, coffee and not a lot of sweetener. As a result, the custard is somewhat bitter. I like that, but you can also add more agave or maple syrup, or use milk chocolate.

SERVES: 4–6
PREP TIME: 15 MINUTES
WAITING TIME: 1 HOUR

GREEN TEA POWDER: you can make green tea powder yourself by grinding your favourite green tea. I use longjing for this, but other green teas are fine too. Make extra – it's delicious with sweet baked goods or on the Tea tofu on page 137. If you don't have a grinder, you can also use store-bought matcha powder.

Custard
150 g (5½ oz) dark chocolate or
    milk chocolate
300 g (10½ oz) silken tofu
2 tablespoons agave syrup or maple syrup
2 g (¼ oz) instant coffee

Crumble
60 g (2 oz) cold butter, cubed
80 g (2¾ oz) all-purpose flour
40 g (1½ oz) light brown sugar
1 tablespoon green tea powder
2 tablespoons black sesame seeds

EQUIPMENT
blender or immersion blender

For the custard, bring a little water to the boil in a pan. Place the chocolate in a heatproof bowl and set the bowl on top of the pan, making sure the bottom of the bowl does not touch the water. Melt the chocolate in the bowl.

Add the melted chocolate, silken tofu, agave syrup or maple syrup and coffee to a blender or the bowl of an immersion blender and puree. Transfer to a bowl, cover and refrigerate for at least 1 hour.

Meanwhile, preheat the oven to 180°C (350°F). Place the butter, flour, sugar, tea powder, sesame seeds and a pinch of salt in a bowl and squeeze/rub with your hands until crumbs of different sizes form. Place the crumbs on a baking paper–lined tray or baking dish and bake for about 25 minutes, until golden brown and crispy. Toss halfway through. Allow to cool to room temperature.

Divide the custard between four to six bowls and spoon over the crumble. You can serve any left-over crumble with ice cream or yoghurt another time.

TOFU PUDDING WITH SAGO AND GREEN TEA

In this dessert I combine two things that horrify some people, but make my heart race. I'm thinking now of my friend Veerle, who sat across from me every night in Taiwan when I ordered tofu pudding for dessert. To make matters worse, I also added sago, a kind of jiggly ball similar to tapioca pearls (you know, from bubble tea). If you are like me, this is absolute heaven in terms of texture. Creamy, pudding-like, squishy, with tasty balls in your mouth. Mmmmm.

SERVES: 4
PREP TIME: 30 MINUTES

600 g (1 lb 5 oz) tofu pudding or silken tofu
50 g (1¾ oz) sago
100 g (3½ oz) dark brown sugar
½ teaspoon vanilla extract
1 teaspoon good-quality green tea
   (e.g. sencha)

EQUIPMENT
steamer or basket

Bring water to the boil in a steamer or a saucepan with a steamer basket. Scoop the tofu pudding or silken tofu into bowls suitable for steaming with a large spoon (you want really big chunks of tofu), and steam the tofu for 15–20 minutes, until warmed through and a little firmer to the touch.

Meanwhile, put the sago in a pan with plenty of water and bring to the boil. Boil the sago for 5 minutes, stirring occasionally. Turn off the heat and leave the sago in the water for 10 minutes. Drain and rinse under cold water.

While everything else is cooking, make a sugar syrup. Add the sugar, vanilla extract, green tea, a pinch of salt and 125 ml (½ cup) of water to a saucepan and bring to the boil. Reduce the heat slightly and let it simmer for about 2 minutes, until everything thickens just a bit. Strain the tea leaves from the sugar syrup and mix the syrup with the sago. Spoon the sago and syrup over the tofu and serve.

TOFU PUDDING WITH GINGER SYRUP

Tofu pudding with sugar or ginger syrup is a classic and very easy Chinese dessert. I often buy pre-made sugar syrup from Choi Kee and spoon it over their tofu pudding. If I feel like it, I make the syrup myself, with ginger and lime leaves mixed in. You can eat the tofu warm or cold, depending on your mood and perhaps the weather.

SERVES: 4
PREP TIME: 15 MINUTES

6 cm (2½ in) piece of ginger
6 lime leaves, crushed
125 g (4½ oz) dark brown sugar
600 g (1 lb 5 oz) tofu pudding

EQUIPMENT
steamer or basket (optional)

Bruise the ginger by placing the side of your knife on it and hitting it really hard with your hand; this will help release the flavour. Slice the ginger and place it in a saucepan with the lime leaf, sugar and 100 ml (3½ fl oz) of water. Bring to the boil, then reduce the heat to low and let simmer for 5–6 minutes, until slightly thickened and syrupy.

Scoop the tofu into bowls with a large spoon (you want really big pieces of tofu). If you like, heat the tofu up. This can be done in the microwave for 1–3 minutes, or by steaming the tofu for 6 minutes in a steamer or a saucepan with a steamer basket. Remove the lime leaves and ginger slices from the ginger syrup, pour the syrup over the tofu pudding and serve.

6

SIDE DISHES

THE PERFECT RICE

I know that rice cookers exist and that many people use their fingers to measure the water when cooking rice. I only use my rice cooker when I eat with more than six people (never), and the finger method just doesn't work for me. This is how I cook rice in a pan.

PREP TIME: 30 MINUTES

rice of your choice

Measure the rice. I use 100 g (3½ oz) per person, which is quite a lot. Rinse the rice in a sieve until the water runs clear. For long-grain (jasmine and basmati), measure 1½ times as much water as rice. For short-grain rice (Korean or Japanese rice), I use a 1:1 ratio.

Add the rice, water and possibly a pinch of salt to a pan (I only use salt with long-grain rice). Bring the water to the boil, reduce the heat and cover. Cook the rice until all the water has evaporated and the rice is tender, about 15 minutes. Turn off the heat and let the rice sit with the lid on for about 10 minutes.

BROCCOLI WITH SESAME OIL

SERVES: 2–3
PREP TIME: 10 MINUTES

1 large head of broccoli
1 teaspoon sesame oil
½ teaspoon salt flakes

Bring a large pot of generously salted water to the boil. Cut the broccoli into small florets and the stalk into slices. If the outer layer of the stalk has hard or brown bits on it, cut those off first.

Put the stalk in the water and cook for 1 minute. Add the florets and cook for 2 minutes. Drain in a colander and leave for 1 minute to continue draining – watery broccoli doesn't taste great. Mix with the sesame oil and salt.

CHINESE DRESSING

This dressing is based on a cold salad with cucumber and enoki that I ate in Singapore. I had it at Oriental Chinese Restaurant, along with the Spring onion tofu from page 130. Since it is about seven hundred degrees in Singapore, this cold meal came at the right time. The dressing is very fresh and has a subtle Sichuan flavour due to the peppercorn oil. You eat the cucumber raw (duh), the enoki you steam for 2–3 minutes. I also often make it with mushrooms (oyster mushrooms or king oyster mushrooms), which I tear into strips and cook for 3 minutes. In the latter case, I use black vinegar instead of rice vinegar, but you can do either: whatever floats your boat. This dressing is also delicious on cold green beans, bok choy (pak choy), bean sprouts or silken tofu. Whatever you use, make sure your ingredients are completely cool so they don't absorb too much of the dressing.

SERVES: 3–4
PREP TIME: 10 MINUTES

1 spring onion (scallion), finely chopped
1 small garlic clove, grated
1 teaspoon grated ginger
3 tablespoons Sichuan peppercorn oil
  (see page 157) or use store-bought
1 tablespoon light soy sauce
3 tablespoons rice vinegar or
  black vinegar
pinch of granulated sugar
finely chopped coriander (cilantro),
  leaves and stems, to serve

EQUIPMENT
kitchen thermometer (optional)

Place the spring onion, garlic and ginger in a heat-resistant bowl.

Heat the Sichuan peppercorn oil in a small pan over medium heat to 180°C (350°F); to check whether it is hot enough, you can throw in a small piece of spring onion. If it immediately starts to sizzle, the oil is ready. Pour the pepper oil over the ingredients in the bowl, stir and let stand until everything has simmered. Add the soy sauce and rice vinegar or black vinegar. Season with the sugar and a pinch of salt.

Mix your salad with a few tablespoons of dressing and coriander.

SIDE DISHES

GINGER GARLIC BUTTER

This butter is delicious on warm vegetables, such as broccoli, green beans, brussels sprouts or blanched spinach. Don't be too strict with quantities here; as long as the ginger and garlic are properly absorbed in the butter, not much can go wrong.

SERVES: 2
PREP TIME: 5 MINUTES

3 cm (1¼ in) piece of ginger, grated
1 garlic clove, cut into wafer-thin slices
a big slice of butter
pinch of MSG

Add the ginger, garlic and butter to a wok or frying pan over medium heat. As soon as everything is bubbling, reduce the heat to low and let simmer gently for about 2 minutes. The garlic should be a very light brown, but not crispy. Turn off the heat and add the MSG and a pinch of salt. Stir the butter through your favourite vegetable.

SICHUAN PEPPERCORN OIL

MAKES: 250 ML (1 CUP)
PREP TIME: 10 MINUTES
WAITING TIME: 1 HOUR

4 tablespoons red or green
    Sichuan peppercorns
250 ml (1 cup) neutral oil

EQUIPMENT
mortar and pestle
plastic squeeze bottle

Heat a frying pan over medium heat and roast the Sichuan peppercorns for 30–60 seconds, until they begin to brown and smell delicious. Crush them lightly in a mortar and transfer to a heatproof bowl.

Wipe the pan clean and heat the oil over medium heat until it begins to simmer. Pour the hot oil over the crushed Sichuan peppercorns and stir. Let cool for about 1 hour. Strain the oil and store it in a plastic squeeze bottle or other sealable container. The oil will stay good for at least a few weeks.

KOREAN DRESSING

This somewhat spicy dressing is delicious on lots of cold vegetables. For example, on blanched bok choy (pak choy) or bean sprouts, raw cucumber or steamed eggplant (aubergine).
Make sure your ingredients are completely cool so they don't absorb too much of the dressing.
You can easily rinse bok choy or bean sprouts under the cold tap to speed up this process.

SERVES: 2–3
PREP TIME: 5 MINUTES

2 spring onions (scallions), chopped

1 garlic clove, grated

1 teaspoon sesame oil

1 tablespoon Korean or light soy sauce

1 teaspoon gochugaru

1 teaspoon toasted sesame seeds

1 teaspoon granulated sugar

Mix the spring onion and garlic with the sesame oil, soy sauce, gochugaru, toasted sesame seeds and sugar. Add some salt if necessary. That's it!

CRISPY EGG

SERVES: 1
PREP TIME: 5 MINUTES

neutral oil, for frying

1 egg

Heat a thick layer of oil in a wok or frying pan over high heat (preferably a wok, as the oil will taste better). Carefully break the egg into the hot oil. Fry the egg for about 2 minutes, spooning hot oil over the edges with a spoon so that they become crispy. Drain on paper towel and serve.

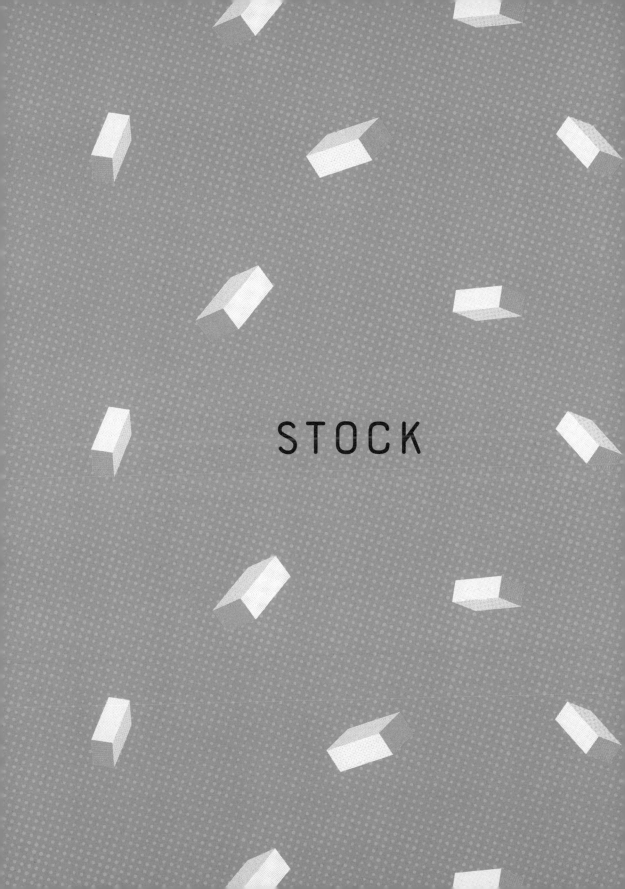

STOCK

CHICKEN STOCK

Homemade stock makes all the difference in dishes. Sometimes I buy stock powder or paste in Asia, but I find cubes from the supermarket downright bad. Because plenty of other seasonings are already used in most dishes, I always prefer to add water instead of stock cubes. Fortunately, stock is made with water.

If you've never made stock from scratch, it seems like a tall order, but all you have to do is toss everything in a pan. I always have chicken stock in my freezer; I boil it way down and store it in a ziplock bag that I cut open with a hot knife before use; you can cut right through the gelatine. I usually make the rest of the stocks in this chapter fresh; they will keep for a week in the fridge.

MAKES 2 LITRES (2 QUARTS)
PREP TIME: 30 MINUTES
WAITING TIME: 2 HOURS

1 kg (2 lb 3 oz) pork bones (optional)

5 spring onions (scallions), chopped into
    5 cm (2 in) pieces

9 cm (3½ in) piece of ginger, sliced

1–2 kg (2 lb 3 oz–4 lb 6 oz) chicken neck,
    carcass and/or wings

10 x 20 cm (4 x 8 in) piece of kombu

1 tablespoon white peppercorns

100 g (3½ oz) prosciutto (optional)

2 teaspoons salt (optional)

If using pork bones, place in a large pot with enough water to cover. Bring to the boil, drain and hold the bones under the tap to rinse off any impurities. Put back in the pan.

Add the rest of the ingredients and about 2.5 litres (2½ quarts) of water to the pan. All the ingredients must be covered by the water. Bring to the boil, reduce the heat to low and simmer gently with the lid on for about 2 hours. Occasionally skim the impurities from the stock with a slotted spoon. Strain the stock.

If you want to freeze the stock, boil it down till only one-quarter remains. Transfer the reduced stock to a ziplock bag, let cool to room temperature and freeze. Dilute the reduced stock with water when you use it. I never add salt, because I prefer to do that when the stock is incorporated into a dish (possibly into salty sauces). If you eat the stock immediately (as a soup, for example), add the salt.

VEGETABLE STOCK

You can follow this recipe exactly, but you can also throw any vegetable scraps you have into a pan of water. Freeze knobs of ginger, the white part of spring onions and other vegetable trimmings. Then you always have something in the kitchen to make homemade stock with.

MAKES: 2 LITRES (2 QUARTS)
PREP TIME: 30 MINUTES
WAITING TIME: 2 HOURS

1 sugarloaf cabbage, quartered
1 carrot, chopped
1 leek, chopped
100 g (3½ oz) ginger, chopped
10 spring onions (scallions), chopped
1 onion, skin-on, quartered
1 teaspoon white peppercorns

Heat a frying pan over high heat – let it get really hot! Roast the cabbage for about 5 minutes on each cut side, until blackened.

Place all the ingredients in a large pan with 2.5 litres (2½ quarts) of water and bring to the boil.

Reduce the heat and let it simmer gently for 1½–2 hours. Check the bubbling status of the stock every now and then: it should always simmer very gently, so that you see a few bubbles. To achieve this, reduce or increase the heat as needed.

Remove all the ingredients from the stock with a slotted spoon or drain the stock over a large saucepan. If you use the stock as a base for soup, season it with plenty of salt. Start with 2 teaspoons, taste and add more if necessary. Stock needs a lot of salt and until enough is added, the stock will taste awful and you'll think it's a failure. When this happens, add more salt. If you use the stock to flavour a dish, do not add salt yet. Only do that in the final dish, so you have better control of the end result.

MUSHROOM WATER

If you really don't feel like making stock, pour some hot water over dried mushrooms and use the mushroom water as stock.

MAKES: 500 ML (2 CUPS)
PREP TIME: 2 MINUTES
WAITING TIME: 1 HOUR

25 g (1 oz) dried shiitake mushrooms

500 ml (2 cups) boiling water

Place the shiitake mushrooms in a heatproof bowl and pour the boiling water over them. Allow to sit for at least 1 hour. Strain and use the water to flavour dishes.

DASHI

MAKES: 200 ML (7 FL OZ)
PREP TIME: 20 MINUTES
WAITING TIME: 30 MINUTES

20 g (¾ oz) kombu
20 g (¾ oz) katsuobushi

Place the kombu in 200 ml (7 fl oz) of cold water in a pan and let it soak for at least 30 minutes.

Bring the water to the boil – as soon as it does, remove the kombu. Add the katsuobushi, season with salt and turn off the heat. Let steep for 2 minutes and strain the dashi.

VEGAN DASHI

MAKES: 200 ML (7 FL OZ)
PREP TIME: 20 MINUTES
WAITING TIME: 30 MINUTES

20 g (¾ oz) kombu
3 shallots, skin-on, halved

Place the kombu in 200 ml (7 fl oz) of cold water in a pan and let it soak for at least 30 minutes. Meanwhile, heat a frying pan over high heat. Place the shallot sliced-side down and place another frying pan on top with something heavy in it (a mortar or tin of beans, for example). Roast the shallot for 7 minutes until completely blackened. Remove from the pan and set aside.

Bring the water with the kombu to the boil – as soon as it boils, remove the kombu. Add the shallot to the water and reduce the heat slightly. Simmer gently for 10–15 minutes. Taste and season with salt (I use about ½ teaspoon for this quantity), then strain the dashi.

CRISPIES

I am happiest when my crispy supply is on point. Of course I always have store-bought fried onions at home, but the crispies that follow really take your dishes to the next level. I often make a lot of them in a row so that I can fry them all in the same oil. Let the crispies cool completely before storing, otherwise they will steam and become soggy. Onion, shallot, garlic and spring onion (scallion) crispies will keep for a week or two in a sealed container; soy and peanut crispies for longer.

ONION, SHALLOT AND GARLIC CRISPIES

Onion, shallot and garlic all have the same cooking time. You can prepare them separately, or together. This combination of cripies is my favourite. Watch out that you don't put too much in the pan at once, otherwise your ingredients won't turn crispy. I usually do three shallots in a medium-sized frying pan.

onions, shallots and/or garlic
neutral oil, for frying
salt flakes

Slice the onions and/or shallots as thinly as possible into rings, with a mandoline if you have one. Slice the garlic. Make sure that all rings and/or slices are equally thin, so that they cook evenly.

Heat the oil in a wok or frying pan over medium heat; there should be enough oil to cover your onion, shallot and/or garlic. Fry for about 10 minutes, until golden brown. Watch out that they don't cook too quickly: the oil should simmer gently the entire time. To achieve this, adjust the heat as needed. Toss regularly.

Drain the onion, shallot and/or garlic in a sieve over a bowl to collect the oil. Place the crispies on a paper towel–lined plate, spread out in one layer, and season with salt flakes. The crispies become even crispier as they cool down.

Save the oil to fry an egg in, to mix through your rice, to pour over vegetables or anything else you can think of. I always keep different types of oil in plastic squeeze bottles in the fridge.

PEANUT CRISPIES

For this recipe, you may have to go to the Asian grocery store for raw peanuts. They are different from regular peanuts and are really a must for peanut crispies.

PREP TIME: 5–10 MINUTES

neutral oil, for frying
raw unsalted peanuts
salt flakes

EQUIPMENT
kitchen thermometer

Heat enough neutral oil in a wok or frying pan so the peanuts will be completely submerged. I prefer to use a wok for this, because then you need less oil. If you have a kitchen thermometer, heat the oil to 170°C (340°F), or until a cube of bread dropped in the oil browns in 20 seconds.

Add the peanuts and fry for about 2 minutes, until golden brown and crispy. Watch out that they don't burn; they will cook a bit after you take them out of the oil. Remove the peanuts from the oil with a slotted spoon and place in one layer on a plate lined with paper towel. Season with salt flakes and let cool completely.

SPRING ONION CRISPIES

PREP TIME: 20 MINUTES

spring onions (scallions)
neutral oil, for frying
salt flakes

Cut the spring onions into thin rings or into 5 cm (2 in) pieces, and then into thin strips. Follow the method for the Onion, shallot and garlic crispies (see page 170), but give the spring onion a little longer: about 12 minutes.

SOY CRISPIES

PREP TIME: 15 MINUTES
WAITING TIME: 8–12 HOURS

dried soybeans
neutral oil, for frying
salt flakes

EQUIPMENT
kitchen thermometer (optional)

Place the soybeans in a bowl full of water and soak for 8–12 hours. Drain and dry well. Heat enough neutral oil in a wok or frying pan to cover the soybeans. I prefer to use a wok for this, because then you need less oil.

Heat the the oil to 180°C (350°F) or until a cube of bread dropped in the oil browns in 15 seconds. Add the soybeans and fry for 5–8 minutes until golden brown and crispy. Remove the soybeans with a slotted spoon and place in one layer on a plate lined with paper towel. Season with salt flakes and let cool completely.

THE VERY BEST CRISPY CHILLI OIL

MAKE: 1 LITRE (1 QUART)
PREP TIME: 20 MINUTES
WAITING TIME: 2 HOURS

MAKE IT VEGAN: omit the fish sauce
and add some extra salt or soy sauce,
if necessary.

950 ml (32 fl oz) neutral oil
9 garlic cloves, 4 sliced, 5 finely chopped
3 shallots, thinly sliced into rings
1 tablespoon Sichuan peppercorns
6 cm (2½ in) piece of ginger, finely chopped
50 g (1¾ oz) gochugaru or dried chilli flakes
1 cinnamon stick
3 star anise
2 tablespoons salt flakes
½ teaspoon MSG
100 ml (3½ fl oz) sesame oil
3 tablespoons light soy sauce
2 tablespoons fish sauce

EQUIPMENT
mortar and pestle or spice/coffee grinder
kitchen thermometer

Heat 200 ml (7 fl oz) of the neutral oil in a frying pan over medium heat and fry the garlic slices and shallot for 10 minutes, until golden brown and crispy. Adjust the heat as needed, so that the oil is constantly simmering and the shallot and garlic don't burn. Drain the oil into a container, set aside, and drain the shallot and garlic on a paper towel–lined plate.

Grind the Sichuan peppercorns in a mortar or grinder. Combine the ground pepper with the chopped garlic, ginger, gochugaru or dried chilli flakes, cinnamon stick, star anise, salt flakes and MSG in a large heatproof bowl. And I mean really large. The oil will bubble, and you don't want it to overflow.

Heat the rest of the neutral oil in a pan or wok to 180°C (350°F), or until a cube of bread dropped in the oil browns in 15 seconds. Pour the hot oil over the ingredients in the bowl. Do this gently and little by little, so that the oil does not overflow. Once the oil stops bubbling, add the oil in which you fried the shallot and garlic, along with the sesame oil, soy sauce and fish sauce. This will prevent the chilli flakes from overcooking and becoming bitter. Let stand for at least 2 hours to allow the flavours to infuse, then add the fried garlic and shallot and mix well. Transfer the crispy chilli oil to jars and store at room temperature.

THANKS

Thank you: Miriam, for all you do without me noticing to make sure every book gets better and better – and that you want to make books with me in the first place; Sofie, for lighting a fire under my ass at exactly the right time, namely just before the deadline; Sophia for the fun, coffee, support, being a rock – oh, and the beautiful photos; Jelle for the fantastic design; Sandra for arranging and thinking about everything; Walter for everything; Xinyu for your ridiculously delicious recipe, the tastiest Sichuan pepper and the cooking inspiration; Tofu girls Chinzy and Janet for your recipe, fun and for making the best tofu in the Netherlands; Dun Yong for lending tableware and selling the best Asian products; Veer for the dishes; Par for the massages; Recipe testers Maartje, Malou, Marieke, Niqué, Partoe (x2 thanks, how happy are you?!); Sofie and Wouter for improving the recipes.

INDEX

First published in Dutch in 2022 by Nijgh Cuisine, Amsterdam
Original title *Emma's Amazing Asia: Tofu*

© 2022 Nijgh Cuisine
Nijgh Cuisine is an imprint of Nijgh & Van Ditmar
www.nijghenvanditmar.nl

Text & recipes: Emma de Thouars
Food styling: Emma de Thouars
Food photography & styling: Sophia van den Hoek, Studio Unfolded
Cover design & layout: Jelle F. Post
Recipe whisperer: Marieke Migchelbrink

This edition published in 2023 by Smith Street Books
Naarm (Melbourne) | Australia | smithstreetbooks.com

ISBN 978-1-9227-5447-9

Smith Street Books respectfully acknowledges the Wurundjeri People of the Kulin Nation, who are the Traditional Owners of the land on which we work, and we pay our respects to their Elders past and present.

For Smith Street Books
English translation: Lucy Grant
Editor: Avery Hayes
Proofreader: Ariana Klepac
Indexer: Helena Holmgren

Printed & bound in China by C&C Offset Printing Co., Ltd.

Book 273
10 9 8 7 6 5 4 3 2 1